A Formal Lexicon
for the Social Sciences

A Formal Lexicon
for the Social Sciences

Robert J. Wolfson

Florida Atlantic University Press

Boca Raton

H.
49.5
W64
1990

The Florida Atlantic University Press is a member of University Presses of Florida, the scholarly publishing agency of the State University System of Florida. Books are selected for publication by faculty editorial committees at each of Florida's nine public universities: Florida A&M University (Tallahassee), Florida Atlantic University (Boca Raton), Florida International University (Miami), Florida State University (Tallahassee), University of Central Florida (Orlando), University of Florida (Gainesville), University of North Florida (Jacksonville), University of South Florida (Tampa), University of West Florida (Pensacola).

Orders for books published by all member presses should be addressed to University Presses of Florida, 15 NW 15th St., Gainesville, FL 32611.

Library of Congress Cataloging-in-Publication Data

Wolfson, Robert J. (Robert Joseph), 1925–
    A formal lexicon for the social sciences / Robert J. Wolfson.
        p.   cm.
    Includes bibliographical references.
    ISBN 0–8130–0978–2 (alk. paper)
    1. Social sciences—Terminology.   I. Title.
H49.5.W64   1990   90–35383
300'.14—dc20   CIP

To Betty

Contents

Acknowledgments

THIS work arose and came to fruition because of two sets of influences. One was the influence of six people on my own intellectual development. The other was the encouragement I have received, especially from one person, which led me to ignore the coolness displayed by most philosophers and social scientists who learned of this work when it was in progress.

My parents, Rose Ladinsky Wolfson and Jacob Wolfson, reared me in an atmosphere of love, intellectual stimulus, and respect for the works of the mind, especially science and the arts. It was their view, and it became mine, that to be a productive scientist was one of the highest callings to which one could aspire.

Herbert G. Bohnert, who was a graduate student in philosophy at the University of Chicago in 1942, when I was in my second year as an undergraduate, introduced me to the works of the Vienna Circle. At that time I expected to become a physicist, and the INTERNATIONAL ENCYCLOPEDIA OF UNIFIED SCIENCE opened new worlds for me. It took some years for me to appreciate them, and to learn how to enter them. Eventually I did learn, and that has led to this work.

Bert F. Hoselitz, of the University of Chicago, was the teacher I encountered in 1947, after I had decided to leave physics and did not know how to pursue my goals. I have always thought of him as the person who found me wandering about in confusion and helped me to sort things out. He guided me into broader reading in the methodology of the social sciences, into the social sciences themselves, and especially into economics. During the years I have pursued this work I have always remembered my experiences in his classes and his office. Of all the years I spent at Chicago, the times I spent with him, as student and as colleague, were intellectually the richest.

Not least important were Richard S. Rudner and Robert B. Barrett, Jr., especially Rudner—our collaboration and friendship began some years earlier than did the collaboration and friendship between Barrett and me. But from both of them I learned much technical philosophy, and a great deal more. Although our collaboration foundered (see the preface) our friendships did not, and I think I know how much I owe them.

Finally, in recent years Joseph C. Pitt has repeatedly urged me to continue this work, and has spoken of it in strongly favorable terms. I am profoundly grateful to him. One doesn't mind talking to one other person, but it is strange to be talking to only oneself. Joe spared me that.

Preface

EARLY in 1958, Richard S. Rudner, a philosopher of science, and I, an economic theorist, then colleagues at Michigan State University, found that we shared some strong interests in the scientific basis of the social sciences.

After some preliminary work in the winter and spring of 1958, we spent that summer at the second Behavioral Science Research Symposium, held at the University of New Mexico and sponsored by the U.S. Air Force Office of Scientific Research. During that summer we planned the development of a constructional system of definitions which, at the time, we hoped to apply to the theory of organizational behavior. With further work during the subsequent year, Rudner and I developed a first set of definitions based on nine primitive terms. That work led to the publication of a paper in 1962 [60] that incorporated a set of definitions—the primitives plus one hundred definitions in four groups: preliminary (21 definitions), decision behavior (26), cooperation and conflict (21), and organization (32).

No further work was done on the project until the summer of 1964 when Rudner (then at Washington University in St. Louis) and I (at the RAND Corporation in Santa Monica) were able to begin work again at RAND. We were joined by Robert B. Barrett, also a member of the Department of Philosophy at Washington University. In this period the old set of definitions was scrapped, and a new one developed, based on a more carefully worked out philosophical basis and a new set of primitives. The three of us worked intensively at RAND during the summers of 1964 and 1965 and intermittently thereafter.

By mid-1966 the basic approach to the project, and construction of many definitions, had been completed, and a RAND working paper [3], which served as basis for parts of the first and middle portions of chapter 1, had been jointly written. From 1967 on it was fiscally and physically more difficult for all three of us to work together. Of even greater importance was the fact, which emerged slowly and incompletely, that we had different views of the project. Apparently Barrett and Rudner began to doubt the feasibility of the attainment of their philosophical goals (of which more later), and although it was not discussed openly, it seems that they found it increasingly difficult to sustain their interest in the project as they saw it. Little more was accomplished before Rudner's death in July 1979.

Barrett and I agreed, after Rudner's death, to complete the work as soon as possible, and we laid out plans for dividing the work of conducting the remaining research and for the writing, chapter by chapter. During 1982 and early 1983 I wrote drafts of most of the chapters for which I had responsibility. However, Barrett's reservations continued to grow, and he neither wrote any of his projected work nor commented on the work I had done. Finally, in a letter written in May 1984, he formally withdrew and renounced all claims to the project. In this letter he suggested, offering convincing supporting evidence, that Rudner had had similar doubts.

In attempting to understand their (from this vantage point obvious) loss of interest in pursuing the project, I have come to some conclusions. The real problem, in all likelihood, was that they were philosophers, not scientists.

Philosophers are more meticulous—more finicky—than scientists are. Messy assumptions and concepts disturb philosophers, while scientists are willing to, and occasionally find it necessary to, cut Gordian knots, make the quick and dirty assumption, etc. Barrett and Rudner were troubled by such matters as the way in which, in our system, we dealt with the matter of belief, which appears as the fifth primitive (P5: individuals that have F believe that p) in chapter 2. As Barrett put it on one occasion, "Why do we strain at gnats about [the way we handle the definition of] organization while we swallow the elephant of belief?"

That sort of thing is one of the messy situations that a scientist is willing to tolerate at an early stage of development of theoretical material, to be cleaned up later on. In similar fashion the physicists made their own deals about quantum mechanics, and philosophers of science came along much later to clean up their messes. But the physicists did not bring the scientific enterprise to a halt until the philosophers were satisfied. My choice was to be messy, when necessary, while attempting to move forward, but Barrett and Rudner were not satisfied with that state of affairs. I believe that it was on this rock that the partnership foundered.

After much thought about the basis on which the project must rest, and some substantial revision of plans, I have continued the project alone. However, it must be understood that a significant portion of the earlier sections of the work reported here was done jointly. Specifically, the three of us, together, wrote much of the material that now appears in the last seven paragraphs of section one and the first seven paragraphs of section two, of chapter 1. In addition, we constructed the primitives and the clarifications in chapter 2 of primitives P1, P2, and P6. The definitions in chapters 3 and 4, and about one-fifth of the definitions in chapter 5 (all of this material originally appeared in [3]) were done by the three of us. Beyond that there was a great deal of inconclusive work on defining concepts related to organizations that we did together. And paragraphs 4–7 of the third section of chapter 1 were written by Barrett and me. This material appeared in [75: 223–25]. But the balance of the work, including the clarifications of primitives P3, P4, and P5, most of the definitions and discussion of conflict, cooperation, and teleologically independent behavior, all of the introductory material in chapters 3–5, the work on contracts, vengeance, etc., and all of the writing except for the middle portion of the introductory chapter, I did alone. I originated and developed the entire conception of computer management of the logical manipulation of theoretical statements that are expressed in terms of these definitions.

The working relationship between Barrett and Rudner, on the one hand, and me, on the other, was not an easy one. But we had a long and largely satisfying friendship, and I learned an immense amount from them. I know that it would have been much more difficult to carry out the work had I not begun it with them.

1

Theories in the Social Sciences: Historical and Methodological Considerations

IN this book, methods are developed and presented whose object is to facilitate the exploration of the logical structure and implications of theories of social behavior. The approach taken is unapologetically materialist and empiricist. More than that, it deals with the scientific theory as an object that is necessarily a linguistic object and that must display certain logical attributes, including internal logical consistency as well as clear, logical connection between the axioms of the theory and the theorems imputed to the theory.

As the book unfolds, the philosophically sophisticated reader may begin to suspect that it is an attempt to resuscitate logical positivism, that intellectual movement long been thought to be dead or in a state of suspended animation. It may appear that there are some similarities between this enterprise and such works as Carnap [5] and Goodman [25], both of which emerged from the logical positivist movement. This book does make use of the constructional definitional system, as do both of these works. But this work is not logical positivism. It does not subscribe to two of the major premises of logical positivism: It does *not* assume that there is possible only one valid theory of any set of phenomena, and it does not assume universal reduction of all scientific theories. Thus, the fact that logical positivism is moribund, if not entirely passé, should not serve as a basis for quick dismissal of this work. If it is to be dismissed, it must be on the grounds that what is proposed is infeasible or worthless, not that it appears, at first glance, to be somehow similar to logical positivism.

This book is confined to an examination of the way in which theories are capable of being tested for logical consistency and empirical implications and to the development of methods. The structure of the processes of social sci-

1

ence theory construction and the empirical testing of social science theories are far beyond its direct concerns.

Historical Background

By the middle of the eighteenth century, some students of individual and social human behavior had begun to think in terms of providing scientific explanations of these phenomena. Their conception of a scientific explanation emulated the most imposing scientific theory then known: Newtonian dynamics. Among these scholars were John Locke and David Hume, especially in their few and scattered economic writings, in the late seventeenth and the mid-eighteenth centuries, and Richard Cantillon, who preceded Adam Smith by about thirty years. Adam Smith, in his two most significant works [64], [65], saw himself as a developer of Newtonian theories of individual and social behavior. For Smith, and for Jeremy Bentham and Thomas Robert Malthus as well, human behavior was explicable in terms of forces (market forces, procreative drives, checks on the increase of human numbers, maximization of utility, etc.) and systems in equilibrium (balance between supply and demand, balance between forces affecting population size, conditions at the margin when utility is maximized, etc.). These fundamental methodological commitments were carried forward by David Ricardo, the utilitarians and philosophical radicals, John Stuart Mill and the neoclassical economists, Auguste Comte, Emile Durkheim, and others up to the present. Each had as a model a slightly different, more modern version of science—in fact of physics.[1]

Nevertheless, despite the proliferation of these ideas and their increasing complexity at the level of social and empirical content, they did not become more sophisticated methodologically. As models of utility maximization, partial and general equilibrium, and theory of the firm developed until the close of the nineteenth century, they fed quite uncritically on the mathematics and models of the physics of two to five decades earlier.

At the same time there developed a growing antipathy to this way of analyzing human behavior. William Godwin, the German historical school of economists (Wilhelm Roscher, Friedrich List, Gustav Schmöller, Max Weber, Werner Sombart), the American institutionalists (Thorstein Veblen, John R. Commons, Wesley C. Mitchell) and their philosophical antecedents, led by Hegel, and other social scientists continuing into the twentieth century be-

---

1. For an interesting insight into recent forms of this fixation of social scientists on physics as a model, see Philip Mirowski [46], [47], [48], [49].

lieved that human existence and institutions are too rich to survive the abstraction of mathematics and even quasi-formal models. The Marxists, while proclaiming themselves as followers of science, had a quite different vision of science than did the Western European and North American empiricists.

I propose, at the risk of oversimplification, to refer to these two groups as the nomological social scientists and the antinomological social scientists and to characterize the focus of this book as an attempt to resolve the major issue between them. The nomological social scientists, while acknowledging that no fully formalized social science theory that is empirically testable has yet emerged, believe that it is a sensible and legitimate objective to try to develop such theories. The antinomological social scientists hold the view that the development of such theories is infeasible, but even if their development were possible they could throw little, if any, light on the behavior of human beings.

Up to this time neither group has demonstrated the validity of its position. The matter is further complicated by the fact that there has really been no agreement between the two groups on how the issue might be settled. For nomological social scientists, the development of successful scientific theories of social phenomena, logically constructed and empirically tested, would constitute support of their position. But support of this kind has yet to be provided.

In economics, the most rigorous and quantitative of the social sciences, there are examples of tightly constructed mathematical or logical theoretical structures. These, however, are built of concepts that do not refer to empirical matter in such a fashion as to permit an empirical test.[2] The central role of utility, in microeconomic theory and increasingly as part of the underpinnings of macroeconomic and general equilibrium theories, hinders empirical testing of economic theory.[3] At the other extreme, in econometrics, there are examples of empirical studies that reveal elaborate empirical regularities in a thoroughly systematic fashion but that are substantially lacking in clear theoretical import, e.g., [31].

In others of the social sciences there have been few empirical regularities discovered and even fewer attempts to account for such as have been found, although there have been conscious attempts to raise the level of systematization. But these efforts have suffered from a variety of failings.

Some have been rather pretentious, confusing formalism with notation

2. E.g., utility in microeconomics and in decision theory and collective choice theory.

3. The economic literature is so vast as to defy citation. Of particular value, however, in reference to this point are [1], [2], [40], [61], [62].

and nothing more. And the notation itself has been quite unperspicuous, not facilitating any use of the apparatus of mathematics or logic (cf. [14]).

Others have ambitiously attempted to construct new concepts that are related to one another in a complex fashion. But they have been expressed in vague and informal terms.[4] This has seriously interfered with the introduction of mathematics or logic and hence has deterred their use in anything resembling formal theoretical work. In addition, their nonintuitive and neologistic character has made it difficult to engage them in the theoretical or empirical work with which social scientists feel comfortable. Moreover, these attempts have been significantly lacking in empirical content, so empirical work has not been much motivated by them.

Another group has borrowed models from such fields as biology and engineering without establishing empirical connections in the field into which they have been imported.[5] Still others have constructed an ordinary language dictionary of important terms in use in the field but have gone no farther toward formalization or systematic interrelation of terms [35].

Thus, in the social sciences we do not find successful instances of the construction or testing of powerful, tightly logical structures of theoretical statements that have significant empirical content.

A frequently expressed concern of antinomological social scientists, such as Winch [71], is that important subtleties of meaning cannot possibly be specified in a formal system. Nomological social scientists claim that, to the contrary, it would indeed be possible to draw far more subtle distinctions, and draw them clearly and precisely, because the components of the terms are plainly visible rather than murkily stated at best, as is generally the case at present. Winch's argument amounts, in essence, to the claim that understanding social phenomena depends, at least in many important cases, on experiencing them. But this seems to the nomological social scientist to make it the responsibility of the social analyst not just to provide scientific explanation of the phenomena but actually to reproduce certain of their features. Thus, as Rudner puts it, Winch's argument commits a rather subtle form of the "reproductive fallacy."[6] The argument, as Rudner unpacks it, seems to rule out all means of gaining knowledge about social phenomena except through direct experience.

Experience and understanding are two distinct concepts. They are not

4. I have the entire Parsonian corpus in mind here. Cf. esp. [53], [54], [55].

5. The attempts to use homeostatic systems and general systems theory in political science, especially by David Easton, e.g., [15], [16], [17].

6. [59: 83].

necessarily identical, nor does either necessarily entail the other. One sort of experience could involve some external stimuli impinging upon the sensory apparatus but not registering consciously. For example, suppose one is sitting in a hall, listening to a lecture. In the background can be heard the noise of the air exhaust system circulating air in and out of the hall. This sound is received by the auditory system but remains part of the background field of stimuli that are received but not noticed. On the other hand, an experience could be the state of affairs in which one knows at the time it occurs that something is happening but cannot offer an explanation of why or how it is happening. That is, the experience may give no insight into causes or consequences. So experience involves stimuli impinging on the sensory receptors, with the experiencer either aware or unaware of that impingement. But in neither case has understanding been gained.

Understanding, on the other hand, is an act of cognition that goes beyond the awareness that it has occurred. It implies the ability to adduce causes and consequences. It is possible, without having experienced some phenomena, to give an account of those phenomena in terms of their causes and consequences; that is, one can understand without experiencing.

This discussion, nomological vs. antinomological, has gone on in philosophy and social science for a number of years, and at many levels.[7] A demonstration of the validity of the case against the possibility of a science of human behavior would consist in the permanent failure of nomological social science. That is, only with a proof of the impossibility of a scientific treatment can the antinomological social scientists' position be thoroughly sustained. This proof has not been offered, and no such proof appears to be in sight. And so the matter is still open.

This book is an attempt to resolve the debate between the nomological and antinomological social scientists by providing the foundation for a theory that meets the nomological social scientists' criteria. It rests on the widely held conception of a scientific theory as a linguistic entity. According to this conception a scientific theory is understood to consist of a set of two sorts of statements about the phenomena that are its subject matter. *Axioms* or *postulates* are general statements about the phenomena that are not subject to proof

---

7. Especially interesting, and at a deep level, is Rorty's Introduction to an anthology on linguistic philosophy in which he explores various types of linguistic philosophy (Ordinary Language Philosophy and Formal Language Philosophy) in their differing forms. He examines, among other issues, the adequacy of formal language in dealing with mundane phenomena and ends the essay with the question of adequacy still open [58: 1–39].

within the theory and are in that sense "assumed." *Theorems* are statements that follow logically from the axioms; that is, they are implied by, deduced from, or provable given the axioms.

For any reasonably rich set of axioms, the total number of significantly distinct theorems that may be inferred can be immense. Empirical testing of such a theory can be carried out by attempting to verify that none of those theorems that are asserted and whose testing is feasible is inconsistent with observable data. If they pass this test, then the theory is supported and normally is accepted. If any of the known and testable theorems of the theory are not sustained, then so long as the scientific community trusts the test procedure the theory may be called into question, dropped, or revised and tested again.

Acceptance of a theory at a given time does not constitute a basis for its unqualified acceptance for all time thereafter. It is the hallmark of empirical science that all theories are, at all times, candidates for rejection or revision. Any of the following occurrences are events that can lead to the questioning of hitherto accepted theories: tests of theorems that were earlier unknown; tests of theorems that were, though known, earlier untestable; and the discovery of or the new understanding of phenomena that were hitherto unknown or differently understood.

Since the components of the scientific theory are statements, they must be constructed of terms. It is with terms that this work is concerned. In effect, what has been begun is the construction of a technical dictionary of terms out of which theories of the social sciences can be built. These terms are of two general sorts. *Primitives* are not defined, but their meaning or content is clarified by example, by ostension, (i.e., demonstratively), or in some other pre-systematic way. *Definitions* are constructed, in a formal logical fashion, of primitives and logical operators plus terms already defined in the field of investigation, as well as primitives or defined terms from logic, mathematics, and empirical sciences more entrenched and better grounded than the one of concern.

At the root of the work reported here lies a question that has frequently been on the minds of nomological social scientists for the past several decades: Why have the social sciences not shown more signs of success as a scientific enterprise? While there are probably other factors involved as well, surely one reason has to do with the nature of the lexicon on which the social sciences—all of them—are based.

In each case that lexicon consists of the natural language plus a sprinkling of technical terminology defined as in a natural language dictionary. There is some variation among fields of the social sciences regarding the extent to which mathematical terminology and modeling are used. But even the mathematics, whatever the nature or extent of it, involves symbols interpreted in the natural language.

These social science lexicons did not then, and still do not today, display any of the definitional structure we see in classical mechanics, which has now become part of chemistry and portions of biology. As Bridgman has so clearly shown [4], all terms in classical mechanics, apart from names and mathematical terms, can in principle be constructed from a primitive base (i.e., a set of primitives) consisting of three terms: mass, length, and time. One consequence of this fact is that there are only three terms in classical mechanics that are clarified primarily by extrasystematic means rather than by being defined within classical mechanics itself. Thus, all other terms are so related to those three primitive terms, and to each other through the primitives, that the process of measurement for each of the defined terms is logically related to the process of measurement for each of the three primitives and thus through them to the processes of measurement of all the others. Consequently there is greater clarity of meaning than is displayed in statements constructed of terms defined as in a natural language dictionary. And there is complete freedom from the circularity of definition that is commonly found in such sets of definitions.

These properties are characteristic of the lexicon of classical mechanics, but they are not present in the lexicon of any of the social sciences. There instead we find that successive uses of the same term by one speaker or writer often involve slightly different meanings. If terms are used by different speakers or writers, the differences in their meanings are no longer slight. Measurement of one concept is not systematically related, through definitional connection, to that of another. Moreover there are vast umbras and penumbras of unclarity. This state of affairs suggests that it would be worthwhile to try to devise a constructional framework for such a system of definitions,[8] one that would be appropriate for some field of the social sciences.

If we look at the terms in which almost any theoretical work in the social sciences is couched, we see that for most of these terms the works as wholes provide no formal explication. Their intelligibility to the reader depends, in

8. "The definitions of an uninterpreted symbolic system serve as mere conventions of notational interchangeability . . . in a constructional system; however, most of the definitions are introduced for explanatory purposes. They may be arbitrary in the sense that they present a choice among alternative definientia (*definitions*), but whatever the choice . . . the definiendum (*what is defined*) . . . is . . . a familiar meaningful term. . . . A constructional definition is correct . . . if the range of application of its definiens is the same as that of its definiendum" (italics added) [25: 3].

large measure, upon what the reader brings to these works from his or her experience of such terms in past discourse, or else it depends upon informal contextual clues that the reader may glean from the occurrences of these terms in the work itself. Thus, key terms remain formally unexplicated in these works.

The contrast furnished by the constructional system that follows could scarcely be more marked. Extant works in social science theory take terms like *power, trust, value, contract, organization, prejudice,* and hundreds or even thousands more, to be antecedently or contextually clear enough already to serve as bases for the explication of additional concepts about social phenomena that they introduce. On the other hand, the constructional system to be laid out in what follows will have the systematic explication of such terms as its objective. This lexicon would be successful if it arrived at a point in clarification that most other works assume, so to speak, as their point of departure. This work, in short, is an examination of foundations: It is quite literally set at a much more fundamental level than has been usual in the social sciences. And, of course, one of its presuppositions is that terms, such as most of those listed above, are antecedently sufficiently unclear to render them inadequate as bases for the construction of further concepts, that is, sufficiently unclear to make a formal attempt at explicating them a worthwhile undertaking.

But a constructional approach differs from the more usual ones in a second way, a way other than the base level at which it cuts in. Not only is the present one in contrast with the usual approaches in respect to what it takes as a basis, but it also contrasts markedly in respect to the degree to which it is rigorous or overtly articulated.

To be sure, virtually every discussion of socioeconomic behavior is constructional to some extent; this is merely to say that virtually all discussions give some explicit indication of the logical structure of, and the logical connections among, at least some of the formulations that comprise them. The contrast provided by this enterprise stems in large measure from the relatively high degree to which the logical structure of, and the logical connections among, its formulations have been explicitly delineated. Concomitantly, it stems also from what might be called the degree of "systematicity" that is a consequence of this. The two characteristics, *degree of systematization* and *degree to which the logical structure of formulations has been explicitly articulated,* are important keys to understanding the nature and efficacy of significantly constructional approaches.

Without, at the outset, giving a full-scale exposition of the notion of the degree to which a set of formulations has been systematized, I may at least indicate that my initial focus of attention here is *not* on the kind of systematization familiarly exemplified by an axiomatic system of *statements*. Instead, attention will be turned to systems of nonstatemental formulations—i.e., to systems of *concepts*, the sort of systems of concepts in particular that standardly constitute definitional systems. Accordingly, this aspect of concern may be characterized as being with the degree of systematization achieved for sets of concepts that serve as the bases of definitional systems, i.e., that achieved for sets constituting the primitive-predicate bases of such systems.

Twenty to thirty years ago substantial progress was made on measures closely related to systematicity (mainly due to the work of Nelson Goodman [22], [23]). This work has issued in the development of a *calculus of structural* (or logical) *simplicity* applicable to sets of concepts serving as the primitive-predicate bases of systems of formulations.[9] The connection of this *calculus of simplicity* with the notion of the degree of systematicity has itself been discussed by Goodman. He points out, for example, that for any theory of any scientific subject matter, "system is achieved just to the extent that the basic vocabulary and set of first principles used in dealing with the given subject matter are simplified. When simplicity of basis vanishes to zero, that is, when no term or principle is derived from any of the others, system also vanishes to zero. Systematization is the same thing as simplification of basis" [22].

In what follows, then, I shall speak of *systematization* and *simplicity of predicate basis* interchangeably, the former always intended to apply to predicate (i.e., conceptual) bases unless (as in the next paragraph) otherwise qualified.

A Definitional Framework

The definitional framework that constitutes this work is a systematization of the second sort. What I will attempt to show is how a relatively numerous set of concepts (which I believe would either be useful in or required by an adequate theory of socioeconomic behavior) is systematically derivable from (that is, is explicitly definable by) a relatively small set of primitive concepts; and I will try to show this by producing rigorously the relevant derivations.

In its present stage, of course, the work introduced here is doubly incomplete. First, it is incomplete because it constitutes a partial treatment of only

9. Applicable also in yielding measures of the simplicity of the primitive-predicate bases of axiomatic systems—though *definitional systems,* rather than the axiomatic systems in which these may come to be embedded, remain our concern here.

the first phase of what, should work of this type be carried on, would constitute a three-phase study. The phases of the study would consist of (1) the
construction of a definitional framework of concepts held to be pivotal in any
adequate theory of socioeconomic behavior, (2) the explicit development of
such a theory or a portion of such a theory as a formally articulated system,
and (3) testing of the developed theory.

In a scientific theory systematization, more broadly construed, is charac-
teristically manifested in two ways: by showing the dependence of the deductively *derived* statements of a theory on the deductively *underived* or primitive or most general statements of the theory, and by showing the dependence
of *derivative concepts* of the theory (that is, the theory's *terms* in contrast to
its statements) on the *primitive* or *basic* or *undefined* concepts of that theory.

The second reason for the tentativeness and incompleteness of the present
system is bound up with the fact that *theory construction* (in this case what
has just been referred to as the second phase) and *concept formation* as attempted in this first phase are clearly not processes that can be carried to
successful completion wholly independently of each other. The proper completion of the present constructional system of definitions must, accordingly,
await the development of the least part of the theoretical system in the axiom-
atized theory of which it, itself, will be only one part. The definitions of this
system must thus be construed as partially (though highly) formalized. The
tentativeness of the present system, for example, is reflected both in what
may well be the nonindependence of its primitive elements and also in the
highly schematic character of some of its definitions.

This second reason brings us to the second of the general characteristics
of constructional systems mentioned above: their very constructionalism.
There is, doubtless, little need to labor the point that failure to make explicit
the logical structure of the concepts and statements contained in a theoretical
system may, and probably usually does, have wholly vitiating effects on attempts to formulate adequate theories. Just to the extent that we fail to know
the logical structure of a theory's concepts or propositions do we fail to know
what are *literally* that theory's implications. And surely this is no trivial failure—to choose *not* to bother with the logical structure of our theoretical
formulations is not merely to express an aesthetic preference for discursive
prose, purple or not, over unexciting formalism. To the contrary, the consequence, the cost, of having a formulation whose implications cannot be
drawn is exactly that we cannot use it to predict or to explain anything: that
we cannot determine what would confirm it or disconfirm it. When we do not
know a theory's implications, we do not know its import, we do not know
what it comes to; in a straightforward sense, we do not know what it is we

are talking about in holding that theory. But the most efficient tool available for exhibiting the requisite logical structure of concepts, perhaps the only adequate tool, *is* symbolic logic: This is the efficacy, the explicit use of formalism in constructionalist treatments.

I hope not to be misunderstood on this point. I am not, of course, maintaining that logical precision is by itself a sufficient condition for adequate theorizing. But when logically precise formulations are defective, they are, usually, clearly so and cleanly so. In this sense constructional systems stand in sharp contrast to those masses of intellectually gelatinous verbiage, anecdotal or impressionistic in character and sprinkled with a few piquant *aperçus,* that sometimes pass as theories of human behavior. The prevalence and especially the persistence of such monuments of intellectual pabulum are due not so much to a history of their success in explaining anything whatever but rather, like the maunderings of fortune-tellers or astrologers, to their being too amorphous to be susceptible to disconfirmation or refutation. In the present constructional system I have tried to avoid the dreadful situation just sketched by explicitly exhibiting the logical structure of the several scores of concepts that have been definitionally introduced.

There *are* some relative disadvantages to constructional systems. But, for the most part, the disadvantages that generally attend the building of a constructional system are just the disadvantages that always accrue (as Bertrand Russell, one of the progenitors of constructionalism, once remarked in a similar context) to honest toil over theft.

The system has some idiosyncratic features. Thus far, having differentiated the system presented here as a *conceptual* rather than a *statemental* constructional system, I have been concerned with the characteristics it shares with other constructional systems: its systematicity and the high degree to which it makes explicit the logical structure of its concepts. But the present system has some peculiarities that also distinguish it from most other constructional systems as well, especially its nominalism and the character of its primitives. These matters will be discussed at greater length in chapter 2.

In applying these definitions to a set of social phenomena, what are the terms to be defined? That is, what are the terms of which theories of social phenomena are (or have to be) constructed?

The preface to this book contains a brief history of this work. Rudner and I made our first attempt to construct a definitional system for the social sciences in 1958–62. The nine primitives used in this first effort were *time-slice, producer-or-potential-producer-of, mechanical class, physical class, morphological class, functional class, event, probability,* and *belief.* Of these the first six were borrowed from work by C. West Churchman and Russell Ackoff [9], [10], who attempted, in the 1940s, to formulate a definitional system for the field of personality psychology.

This first set of definitions was never applied, not even loosely or super-ficially, to any body of theoretical discourse, and after the publication of these results [60] events interfered for a while with further activity. Beginning in the summer of 1964, Rudner and I, joined in 1965 by Barrett, began work on a substantial revision of the earlier definitional system.

As we resumed our work we gave much thought to the differences be-tween the "nominalist" and "Platonist" approaches to logic to which Nelson Goodman points [21], [26]. Goodman asserts that severe ontological prob-lems arise from the fact that, for purposes of constructing formal existential statements, Platonists (i.e., users of the calculus of classes) do not discrimi-nate among individuals, classes of individuals, classes of classes, and so on. As Goodman puts it:

> Use of the calculus of classes, once we have admitted any individuals at all, opens the door to all classes, classes of classes, etc., of those individuals, and so may import, in addition to the individuals pur-posely admitted by our choice of the special primitives, an infinite multitude of other entities that are not individual. Supposedly innocent machinery may in this way be responsible for more of the ontology than are frankly "empirical" primitives. . . . The nominalistically minded philosopher like myself will not willingly use apparatus that peoples his world with a host of ethereal, platonic, pseudo entities. As a result he will so far as he can avoid all use of the calculus of classes, and every other reference to non-individuals in constructing a system. [25: 25–26]

We found this argument persuasive, so we decided to formulate our defi-nitions nominalistically. Consequently, we used the calculus of individuals, a nominalist form of logic developed by Goodman, Henry S. Leonard, and W. V. O. Quine [26], [36] that, in contrast to much standard logic, permits existential statements to be made only at the lowest level of abstraction (the level of individuals)[10] and not simultaneously about abstract ideas. Thus,

10. "Individual" is here understood as any tangible material object or collection thereof (where "object" is construed to include organisms—humans, animals, etc.) or any part of an individual. An individual, if it is a collection of individuals, need not be homogeneous. That is, while a group of people, or a group of chairs, or a group

statements like "there is a sweater" (a claim that a sweater exists) can be made in nominalist logic. But in nominalist logic one cannot also say "there is a heaviness" (that is, that the weight of an object exists in any sense independently of the object). "Heaviness," as it is frequently used in ordinary speech and in Platonist logic, appears to refer to an idea or essence that approaches, but does not achieve, existence when it is an attribute of an individual. On the other hand, "sweater" refers to an object or individual. "This heaviness exists" is not the same sort of expression as "this sweater exists." In contrast to nominalist logic, much standard logic admits treatment of symbols referring to abstractions in just the same way as it treats symbols referring to individuals. Consequently nominalists speak of such standard logic as "Platonist logic," in reference to the central place of ideas or essences in Plato's philosophy.

To be sure, there are heavy costs imposed by this decision. Much of mathematics becomes less available, and formal expressions become more unwieldy.[11] Indeed, it may be that it will turn out not to be worthwhile to stay on the nominalist path. But on the other hand a recent monograph [20] holds out the prospect that it may not be necessary to abandon nominalism. Moreover, as the constructional system is adapted for use on the modern computer, it becomes more and more apparent that the computer imposes a strong pressure toward nominalist logic because of its requirement that variables covered by quantification be completely constructed.

A by-product of this decision to couch our definitions in nominalist terms is that the possibility was left open, although it was remote at the time the decision was made, of automatic proof of theorems. In principle, computing algorithms might be used to prove theorems. At least, the character of the underlying logic implied by this ontological commitment does not preclude such a possibility from the start.

---

of human legs (amputated or not), or a group of chair rungs (necessarily separate from functioning chairs) can be an individual, so can a collection consisting of a chair leg, five fingers (three still on a live hand), and a book, for example. (Goodman has since clarified his personal conception of "individual" in such a way as to extend it well beyond the physical to abstract entities of many sorts so long as they lack the formal characteristics of classes. But we did not follow his lead here.)

11. As we have seen, Goodman rests his case for nominalism on the "ethereal, platonic" nature of "classes, classes of classes," etc. Almost all the techniques of modern mathematical analysis, including the theory of functions and topology, and most proof techniques, involve the use of sets (classes), sets of sets, etc. Consequently, only to the extent that the Brouwer-Robinson program in mathematics succeeds can many modern mathematical tools be freely available to a nominalist.

In this second version of the system we reformulated our primitives, reduced their number to six, and nominalized them. Using these six primitives we began the construction of four groups of definitions: auxiliary, decision, socioeconomic, and organization. Of these four groups the last, organizational definitions, are in need of much reworking and have not been included in this book.[12] (The problems in dealing with organizational definitions are discussed in chapter 6.)

The test of a primitive basis for a formal definitional schema should concern itself with three questions. Can a set of terms referring to concepts concerning a major group of phenomena be defined out of this primitive basis? Does this set of definitions naturally extend to concepts concerned with related groups of phenomena?[13] Is the set of primitives small enough in number, relative to the number of concepts to be defined out of it, that the resulting vocabulary constitutes a systematically related set of concepts? That is, do the definitions display a high degree of systematicity (i.e., simplicity)?

There is reason to feel that both sets of primitives pass all these tests. In both versions the decision to stop constructing definitions came not because of the difficulty of construction but rather because it became clear that more definitions could be constructed when and as needed. Moreover, it seems clear to me that not only has it been possible to construct definitions for such terms as *decision, cooperation, conflict, preference,* etc., but that it can easily be seen how definitions for many more concepts could be formulated. And the entire structure is built up out of six extralogical primitives (i.e., six primitives that are concerned with empirical substance and not with the apparatus of logic).

The decision to construct a formal lexicon for a field of the social sciences entails a commitment to provide a lexicon in which a framework or schematism for all theoretical statements of that field (i.e., all axioms or postulates and, consequently, assuming full formalization of all theories, all theorems dealing with any portion of that field) could be constructed. That is, successful completion of this task should facilitate the conduct of all formal scientific discourse in the field in a lexicon consisting of defined terms and the primitives, plus some logic and mathematics and terms from other mature sciences, plus the names of individuals (i.e., elementary objects of the field), in place of the natural language.

12. This was as far as our joint effort went.
13. Connectibility of theories dealing with conceptually adjacent fields is a desirable characteristic. It aids in the generalization of theories.

Methodological Considerations

A large claim has been made, namely, that this work will attempt to provide formal tools for the construction, testing, and utilization of theories in the social sciences. The announcement of such a project raises a number of contentious issues in contemporary philosophy of science. Many readers might understand, in view of philosophical developments during the past three decades,[14] that such a project as this is founded on philosophical positions long since shown to be unsound. I will attempt to show that while at first glance it might seem that this project rests on some of the primary assumptions underlying logical positivism, that is not the case; the criticisms that laid logical positivism low do not apply here.

Furthermore, no clear statement has yet been offered of the range of social sciences that might be affected or how they would be related to one another, if at all. At the end of this chapter, I will sketch out the social terrain over which we will be traveling.

One of the great influences in twentieth-century philosophy of science has been logical positivism. For as long as they dominated Western analytic philosophy, the logical positivists aimed at the Unification of the Sciences.[15] They intended this in two senses. First, there was the claim that there is one correct theory of any given set of phenomena. Second, there was the claim that the ultimate objective of the program was to unearth, for each range of phenomena, the one correct theory and then to assemble all these theories (which, since they deal with ranges of interrelated phenomena, can themselves be interrelated) into a complete hierarchy expressed in one set of terms. In other words all phenomena, whether social, psychological, biological, geological, chemical, or meteorological, could be described in terms of the most fundamental (probably microphysical) concepts. This conception was one of universal reductionism.

It may immediately occur to the reader of this work that a definitional system of the general type being proposed in this work has normally served as an adjunct to a formalized scientific theory, which is to say a theory expressed as a formal axiomatic system in a formalized language with an under-

---

14. I refer to the decline of logical positivism as a leading position of influence in the philosophy of science.

15. Here capitalized because it was under this banner that the Vienna Circle, the originators of that intellectual movement, mobilized. Cf., for example, the publishing program carried out under the title *International Encyclopedia of Unified Science* [30].

lying logic of the kind just alluded to. Scientific theories construed in this fashion may well seem to be a thing of the past that enjoyed a brief heyday in the work of Rudolf Carnap,[16] in some of the earlier work of Carl G. Hempel [29], and in some of the work of other "logical positivists" or "logical empiricists."[17] But that program is now at least quiescent, if not moribund. Therefore, it would probably be appropriate to explain just how this work does not imply a commitment to that earlier program.

In those earlier days the development of an axiomatic basis for scientific theory was linked to a number of specific theses about the nature of the world and of correctly formulated scientific theories about it. Not only was there the "Unity of Science" doctrine in both of the senses discussed above. There was also the belief that a sharp distinction could be drawn between concepts and their interrelations, on the one hand, and matters of fact about the world, on the other. There flowed from this the belief that the conceptual foundations of a theory, the lexicon out of which it is constructed, might be developed a priori, in relative isolation from the conclusions arising out of empirical research.

It is often taken for granted that these and other doctrines like them are presuppositions of an enterprise such as this one, and investigators committed to such projects are often attacked in those terms. But it should be noted carefully that the connections between the formal approach and any of these theses that are historically associated with it are loose, tenuous, and accidental. Theories that are narrowly circumscribed in their subject matter are just as amenable to axiomatization as is a universal scientific theory (i.e., Unified Science), probably more so. Furthermore, the move to axiomatization need not presuppose that some particular axiomatization is the uniquely correct version for that set of phenomena with which it deals. Indeed, there may be many alternatives, the selection among which is made solely on pragmatic grounds. The formal system should be understood to play a role such as that of a mathematical model of a theory or the underlying or implicit logical structure of the theory. It may even simply be the way in which the theory is best understood by the logical analyst, while each of a number of other concerned specialists, the historian of science, the subject matter empirical specialist, or the subject matter theorist, may find it convenient to construe the theory in quite different terms. Finally, a formal lexicon could even be thought of as not being an adjunct to the theory at all. It may be taken simply

16. Much of his work, but most clearly in the appendixes of [6].
17. Notably Hans Reichenbach, A. J. Ayer, Herbert Feigl, Karl Popper, the younger Ludwig Wittgenstein.

as a source of rigorously specified interconceptual relations holding among concepts of quite ordinary, not even formal, kind: a formal court of appeal vis-à-vis otherwise informal notions much like arithmetic in its common role as final arbiter of the accuracy of estimates, approximations, and certain qualitative appraisals.

Yet another aspect of the Unity of Science movement must be dealt with in establishing the methodological position of this enterprise. One goal of the movement was rational reconstruction. Logical positivism aimed at a clear statement of the epistemic foundations of existent scientific theories.[18] That is, this epistemic clarification was to be furnished after the development of these theories. This project, in contrast, is in part concerned with providing means for the formulation of testable statements that can serve as statements of yet-to-be-developed scientific theories. Thus, this work is *not* concerned with rational reconstruction at all.

Not so readily dismissed is the charge that this project does presuppose a not-altogether-discredited doctrine concerning the separation of the conceptual from the factual. How can I undertake to develop, here and now, the vocabulary for a not-yet-fully-mature theory, as though suitable vocabularies were not heavily dependent on empirical results and could be cooked up in advance of those results?

Feyerabend asserts that the meanings of terms used in the axioms of a theory are necessarily totally dependent on the theory itself [19]. The import of this claim is that the meaning of any term used in science is determined by the nature of the theory in which it is used. Thus, if Feyerabend is correct (which is a matter of considerable dispute), a given term would necessarily have different meanings in different theories. Obvious counterexamples are to be found in mathematics. Consider the concept of addition. It is understood in the same way in almost all contexts in which it appears, irrespective of the particular theoretical or empirical situation.

Feyerabend's argument is made with reference to empirical concepts that have not been the object of formal definitional analysis as they came to be used in science. In each theory in which they were used, they were clothed (explicitly in some cases, implicitly in others) with meaning peculiar to the theory in question. But these events are matters of history, not of necessity. Nothing prevents a formal undertaking to the effect that term *x*, when used scientifically in whatever theory, will always be understood in a certain way—perhaps in a way consistent with its definition in a lexicon of the sort being discussed here.

18. This aspect of the logical positivist program was most clearly laid out in [5].

But Feyerabend's position on the dependency of terms on their theories (in my view quite mistaken) should not be confused with a superficially similar, though in fact quite distinct, point. That point, alluded to a few paragraphs ago, is that an empirical theory can scarcely be expected to be entirely couched in terms that have been decided upon in advance and that therefore depend in no way on the empirical content of the theory. Obviously enough, the character that the subject matter covered by the theory is found to have must be allowed some significant role as a determinant of the vocabulary to be used in describing it and theorizing about it. Nor does this development overlook this point. I have made reference to this lexicon as a "constructional framework," which is to say that it purports to provide the skeletal contours of the vocabulary in which a theory using it will be couched but does not claim to enumerate every last term such a theory may appropriately employ. It defines many key terms that will probably prove central to a theory concerned with social phenomena. And it defines schematic structures that probably underlie a number of others. But as the discussion below, of the primitives and a few pivotal defined terms, makes apparent, enormous scope is left to the theory constructor to augment this framework with additional concepts. Wherever a sentence letter, an individual constant letter, or a predicate letter occurs in any of the primitives or defined expressions, an actual sentence, or name, or predicate would have to be supplied by the theory constructor in case of an actual use of that portion of the lexicon in an actual theory. Indeed it is this feature that opens the door to terms from logic, mathematics, and other sciences whose use as part of the lexicon was mentioned earlier.

So far as reductionism is concerned, there is certainly no commitment here to universal reductionism of the sort envisioned by the Vienna Circle. But insofar as different theories of the social sciences are concerned with a given set, or overlapping sets, or related sets, of phenomena (including even sets of phenomena whose relationship may emerge only as work proceeds), to that extent it may turn out to be useful for the possibility of some local or limited reduction to emerge. Two apparently disparate theories could conceivably deal with apparently unrelated or distantly related phenomena in terms of apparently different concepts. But if at a sufficiently deep definitional level it turns out that the same set of primitive (or relatively primitive) terms provides a basis for the construction of both sets of concepts, then a lateral connection has been established—reduction is possible, and unification of those theories can take place. However, it would be a valid unification (assuming no logical errors) only if both theories pass the relevant empirical tests, i.e., only if both theories are accepted on empirical grounds.

Another commitment that I make, a methodological one which is in no way necessary for the development and application of a constructional system of social science theories, is that of methodological individualism. I reject the view, associated with a wide range of social thinkers ranging from Plato through Hegel, Marx, and Durkheim to some of the present day, that social entities encompassing pluralities of human beings cannot be understood as the sum of the individuals involved in them and their relationships with one another, that social entities are emergent phenomena. That is to say, I reject holism and the organic conception of society. I believe that this commitment to methodological individualism makes the connections between the several subfields of the social sciences much more accessible and visible, and the boundaries between these subfields much more penetrable, than would be the case if a holistic view were accepted.

The use of a formal lexicon or lexicons in no way entails a commitment to methodological individualism. Holistic theories are equally receptive to formal treatment as are individualist theories. It is worthwhile to note, however, that holistic theories are much less likely to be reducible into one another and, therefore, are more likely to require the use of distinct lexicons than are individualist theories. But this matter aside, it should be clear that the use of constructional frameworks of concept definition and methodological individualism are orthogonal assumptions. They are independent of one another.

In sum, the present work aims at providing means for the formulation of testable statements, statements that are logically testable, with clear empirical content, that would comprise theories of social phenomena. While this work is not inconsistent with the logical positivist program, it is not a part of that program. It is equally consistent with other programs that are not methodologically individualist, not reductionist, and that do not assume a unique correct theory.

The Social Range

With these matters out of the way, we now look at the social matter that might be explored with these instruments. Aside from the preliminaries covered in the two chapters immediately following, which areas of individual and social behavior will we explore in subsequent chapters, and how do they lead into one another?

What is it that is peculiarly human about human behavior, human in contrast with the sort of thing that happens when the factors that govern are strictly biological, chemical, or physical? Put in another way, how would the social world be different if all consequences of voluntary human action were eliminated? If it were possible to erase all voluntary human actions and their consequences, what would be left of human behavior? Clearly, all decisions, and all action that could be called purposive, would disappear. Moreover, all situations involving more than one human being, at least some of whom are engaged in purposive behavior, in which conflict or cooperation emerged as a consequence of individual purposive behaviors, would also disappear. This would be so whether the interaction of these persons came about as a consequence of explicit or implicit stable arrangements among these persons, i.e., whether it would be appropriate to speak of formal or informal organization.

It is obvious, then, that for a methodological individualist there are clear dependencies, which might imply the usefulness of the limited reductionist position discussed earlier, among levels of human behavior. Individual purposive behavior, i.e., behavior that implies underlying decision(s); cooperative, conflictful, and teleologically independent interactions among persons, some or all of whom are engaged in purposive behavior; explicit or implicit stable arrangements governing or facilitating such interactions, arrangements that might be referred to under the general heading of "organization," may all conceivably be spoken of in terms of behavior. And if we consider it reasonable to remark that family, party, government, nation, voluntary organization, business firm, and even society are all forms of organization, then we can see that a system of formal definitions that begins with individual purposive behavior could conceivably deal with almost everything with which the social sciences deal.

In chapters 2 and 3 we develop tools—primitive terms and auxiliary definitions. In chapter 4 we develop a number of definitions concerned with individual behavior. The centerpiece of that chapter is the notion of purposive behavior or decision behavior. In chapter 5 we deal with interpersonal behavior: cooperation, conflict, and teleologically independent behavior. These are carried through many variations, including such notions as rivalry, competition, aggression, ambush, revenge, etc. Then the notions of expectation and contract are developed. In chapter 6 some problems in defining *organization* are discussed. Implications and possible uses of this work are discussed in chapter 7.

Appendix A discusses the notation used throughout the book. Appendix B lists the primitives discussed in chapter 2. Appendices C, E, and G list the terms defined and discussed in chapters 3, 4, and 5, respectively. In the chapters themselves, the definitions are presented in the following fashion: First the definitions are labeled (AUX for auxiliary terms, DEC for decision terms, and SOC for socioeconomic terms). Within each group the definitions are numbered. Then the "reading" of the formal definiens is given. This reading is an ordinary language clause or phrase that conveys the import of the definition. Then the definiendum is given in what might be called semiformal form. This consists of a reading of the formal definiens, constructed of the readings of the component definitions, connected by the ordinary language equivalents of the logical connectives that appear in the formal definitions (*not, or, and, if . . . then, if and only if, for all x, there is an x,* etc.).

In Appendices D, F, and H, the material presented for each definition in the body of chapters 3, 4, and 5, respectively, is repeated, but in addition the definiens and the definiendum for each defined term appear in formal logical notation. This notation allows the terms defined in the text to be loaded into a logic-theorem prover (a computer running under OTTER 1.0 or similar logic program)[19] for manipulation, consistency checking of a set of axioms, and/or derivation of implications of a set of axioms expressed in this lexicon.

19. OTTER 1.0, a high-speed noninteractive theorem prover, is a software package developed by William McCune of the Applied Mathematics Group at the Argonne National Laboratory. It appears to be a most promising instrument for the examination of such logical structures as theoretical structures built of these formal renderings. OTTER 1.0 has been prepared for use on any computer running under UNIX, of at least the scale of the IBM PC-AT. Moreover, it can run on an AT or AT clone, running under DOS. In addition, there are several other such logic-theorem provers being developed at other institutions.

2

Primitive Terms

THE development of a constructional system, the sort of task here under-
taken, must begin with the selection of a set of primitive (that is, undefined)
terms. These terms must be independent of one another (i.e., in some sense,
orthogonal) and must span the concept space we are trying to cover with the
definitions.

In addition to the logic and vocabulary of *Principia Mathematica* [70],
which serves as the underlying logic of the lexicon, but not including the
epsilon symbol or any of the set-theoretic vocabulary introducible by definition in terms of it, we employ a set of primitive expressions consisting of six
terms. Of these, the first deals with the part-whole relationship in a nominalistic manner. The second provides the basis for temporal ordering of events.
The third allows us to draw empirical distinctions and to develop a basis for
classifying observations. The fourth deals with influences among events and
statements. The fifth deals with beliefs of actors who are being observed. The
sixth provides a basis for making inferences about possibilities, or tendencies
or dispositions of objects to manifest certain behaviors or attributes even
though they have not yet been manifest. These primitive terms are listed
below, along with suggested readings of them, presystematic explanations of
their meanings, and, where appropriate, supplementary discussions of their
roles and importance to the lexicon as a whole.

P1   **overlaps**(x,y) may be read as *x overlaps y*

This two-place predicate holds between a pair of entities just in case they
have a part in common. For example, suppose x to be the Midwest and y to

be the Wheat Belt. Then *x overlaps y* is true, since the two entities in question have Kansas and Nebraska in common.

The "overlaps" predicate is the single extralogical primitive of Goodman, Leonard, and Quine's so-called calculus of individuals [26], [36], which is thus incorporated along with it. Incorporation of that calculus is the result of the choice, alluded to earlier, to exclude set theory and thereby to employ the formally weakest machinery that is compatible with the construction of an adequately serviceable lexicon. For the formally weaker the basis, the less restricted will be the system generated from it (provided, to be sure, that the desired system can be generated at all by these means). And systematicity is what is mainly being sought, the value of the formal constructions in the first place. Set theory is a most powerful extension of logic, so strong, for example, that all of classical mathematics can be reduced to it (or at least reconstructed in it). It was therefore rejected as a matter of course. On the other hand, the unaided logic of *Principia Mathematica* proved too weak for the purposes at hand. Thus, the calculus of individuals was selected, which appears to have proven strong enough for the task while avoiding the ontological and other excesses of set theory. Its choice over set theory amounts to a commitment to nominalism.

Although the nominalism in question limits to individuals the kinds of things embraced in one's ontology, they are "individuals" in a broader sense than the ordinary one. As pointed out in chapter one, not only do spatiotemporally compact entities like persons, houses, books, and trees count as individuals, but so do spatially discontinuous entities like the United States (whose forty-ninth and fiftieth states are noncontiguous with one another and with the remainder), temporally discontinuous entities like the summer heat in St. Louis (which exists for about three months each year but does not for the remaining nine), and spatiotemporally discontinuous entities like the editorial board of the philosophical journal *The Monist* (which existed from 1888 through 1937 and then again, after a period of nonexistence, from 1963 until the present, and when it does exist, consists at various times of several different and therefore normally spatially noncontiguous persons). These temporally discontinuous cases bear a resemblance to the problem of the state of existence of elementary particles in the Copenhagen interpretation of quantum mechanics, credited largely to Niels Bohr and which is the most widely accepted view among physicists of the state of existence of these particles.[1]

1. In that case the problem has to do with whether or not deterministic relationships exist for elementary particles. The Copenhagen interpretation proposes that deterministic statements can properly be made about the probability distributions that describe the wave aspects of the particles, while statements about the particles them-

In an example just as veridical as the Midwest/Wheat Belt illustration given above, the entity that is the sum of the left hands of all presidents of the United States overlaps Theodore Roosevelt, since the two have Roosevelt's left hand as a common part.

P2   **e_slice**(x,y) may be read as *x is an earlier time-slice than y*

This two-place predicate holds between a pair of time-slices just in case the first-mentioned is temporally prior to the second-mentioned. A time-slice is an instantaneous cross section of the universe, that is, it is the entire world and all the physical objects in it at a particular instant in time. It has extensions in three spatial dimensions but no duration at all.

P2 is the basic temporal concept of the definitional system. It makes possible the introduction of such entities as time-slices as well as continuous sequences of time-slices, which form time-intervals. Moreover, with this primitive we are able to construct such notions as a slice-part of an individual, or that region of a time-slice that overlaps an individual, and an interval-part of an individual, that region of a time-interval that overlaps an individual. A slice-part of an individual is thus that individual at a particular instant in time, and an interval-part of an individual is that individual during the interval in question. Of course, a crucial function of this primitive is that it enables us to construct such temporal relations among entities as we may require.

P3   **morph_id**(x,y) may be read as *x is morphologically identical*
      to y

This two-place predicate holds between a pair of individuals just in case they satisfy all the same morphological predicates of the theoretical language. To say that two objects or individuals are morphologically identical, then, is to say that both have the same relevant morphological characteristics. That is, if one member of a pair of morphologically identical individuals satisfies a given relevant morphological predicate, then so does the other. For an individual to satisfy a morphological predicate is for that individual to be partially described by being classified in a range. "Has an income of $100,000 a year" is not a morphological predicate, since it does not refer to a range.

---

selves involve degrees of indeterminacy. In some statements this indeterminacy extends even to the question of the very existence of these particles during the time periods between observations of them.

But "has an income of between \$75,000 and \$119,999," since it refers to a range, is a morphological predicate.

Suppose that all possible incomes were covered by a set of nonoverlapping income ranges. With each of these is then associated a morphological predicate, forming the set of morphological predicates "low income," "middle income," and "high income" (associated with, say, incomes under \$13,000, incomes from \$13,000 to \$29,999, and incomes of \$30,000 and over, respectively). Moreover, let us assume that there is no other predicate in the theoretical language by which individuals are classified into ranges (i.e., there is no other morphological predicate in the language). Then, two individuals are morphologically identical if they fall into the same income range (i.e., if they both satisfy the same predicate from the set "low income," "middle income," or "high income").

Let us now consider a theoretical language containing these three income predicates as well as three additional morphological predicates: "low IQ," "middle IQ," and "high IQ." Individuals are said to satisfy these predicates on the basis of their performance on the Wechsler-Bellevue Intelligence Test (Wechsler-Bellevue score under 70, from 70 to 130 inclusive, and score above 130, respectively). If these are the only two scales in the theoretical language that generate morphological predicates, then two individuals are said to be morphologically identical if they satisfy identical morphological predicates (and each would satisfy exactly two). Otherwise they are said to be morphologically distinct. In general, two individuals are morphologically identical just in case every relevant morphological predicate that one individual satisfies is satisfied by the other, and vice versa.

P4   **con**(x,p) may be read as *x conduces to p*

This one-place predicate holds of some event x just in case some true sentence about x confirms an explanans of which p is the explanandum. That is, event x conduces to the truth of statement p (in some sense helps to bring about the state of affairs described by p) if and only if the explanation of statement p is confirmed by some true sentence about x. Hence, in this context "conducing" means that some true statement about x provides the investigator with some reason to accept statement p as true.

We can clarify the reading of P4, *x conduces to p,* as follows: (S is a true statement about event x) *and* (R is an explanation of statement p) *and* (R is confirmed by S). Thus, the occurrence of x entails the truth of S. But if S is true, then R is confirmed. And R's confirmation explains p. So there is a chain of occurrence, truth, confirmation, and explanation that runs from x to p, as shown below.

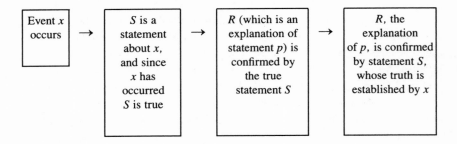

Consider the following example. Let p be the statement

A hyperinflation is likely to occur if an economically complex and liberal country loses a large-scale, bitterly fought war.

Statement p is explained by the following five sentences (the explanation R):

1. A probable result of a large-scale, bitterly fought war is the physical devastation of the labor pool and of the economy.
2. A further likely aftermath of such a war is the imposition of war penalties such as reparations, military occupation, control of economic activity, etc., which seriously interfere with the rapid restoration of the economy.
3. As a consequence, shortages of all sorts of goods and services develop and prices rise.
4. Only if draconian measures are taken by the government can these price increases be kept from accelerating.
5. Draconian measures are difficult for the government of an economically liberal or populist country to impose.

Let event x be the following developments in Germany during the period 1914–1923:

a. Germany was an economically complex, liberal country.
b. Germany engaged in a large-scale, bitterly fought war.
c. Germany's labor pool was devastated in that war.

d. Heavy damage to Germany's physical plant resulted from that war.

e. Germany lost that war.

f. The victors imposed heavy reparations on Germany.

g. The victors occupied part of Germany by military force.

h. The victors imposed stringent economic controls on Germany.

A true statement S about this sequence of developments, event x, is

> In the face of these events the postwar German government, in attempting to deal in a nondraconian manner with the severe shortages of goods and services, allowed the quantity of money to rise rapidly. The result was increasingly higher rates of price inflation.

Thus, it is proper to say that x conduces to p; that is, the fact that the component developments in event x have occurred (S is a true statement) makes more plausible the explanation (R) of p. P4 is the basic confirmation relation of the system. Explication of such notions as *causation, influence,* and *function,* insofar as they enter into the system, are introduced by means of this primitive.

P5   **bel(F,p)** may be read as *individuals that have* **F** *believe that p*

This sentence schema is true for a given choice of predicate F and statement p just in case the predicate F is manifest and an individual's satisfying it is accepted by the investigator as a sufficient condition for the individual's believing that p is true.

Suppose the predicate F is understood as "genuflects upon entering a Roman Catholic church" while p is the statement "the pope is the vicar of Christ on earth." P5 would now read "individuals who genuflect upon entering a Roman Catholic church are construed by the investigator to believe that the pope is the vicar of Christ on earth." This schema serves to define a particular belief (which we usually understand to be a mental state) by associating statements about it with a manifest predicate (a predicate whose satisfaction in a given case may readily be noted by direct observation). That is, in this theoretical language genuflection upon entering a Roman Catholic church would be seen by the investigator as grounds for saying the individual in question believes the pope is Christ's vicar on earth. In another, more complete language there might be several manifest predicates (e.g., in addition to F, perhaps D, "dips hand in holy water font upon entering a Roman Catholic church," or c, "carries rosary into church," etc.) any one (or any *n*) of which being satisfied is taken by the investigator as grounds for saying the belief is held by the subject individual. All notions involving belief, such as the veridical/nonveridical distinction and the subjective/objective distinction, that are used in the definitional system are introduced by means of this primitive.

It should be noted that $-\textbf{bel}(\text{F},\text{p})$ does not imply $\textbf{bel}(\text{F},-\text{p})$. Neither does $\textbf{bel}(\text{F},-\text{p})$ imply $-\textbf{bel}(\text{F},\text{p})$. It is conceivable that F does not believe that *p* because F does not have enough information about *p* to hold any belief at all about *p*.

P6   **index**(x,**F**) may be read as *x satisfies an index of* **F**

This one-place predicate is true of any individual for any choice of predicate just in case the individual satisfies an index of the predicate. An *index of a predicate* is another predicate, a manifest one, that is satisfied by everything satisfying the former and by some other things besides, where there is theoretical justification for holding that these other things would have F too, under appropriate circumstances.

Suppose *x* is a phonograph record and R is the manifest predicate "is being played." Then R*x* can be read "phonograph record *x* is being played." Consider the phonograph record *y*, which is not being played. That is, *y* does not satisfy the manifest predicate R. But if P is the dispositional predicate "is playable," can we determine on what grounds we might be justified in saying that *y* has P?

We might examine the record *x*, the record that is actually being played, and find that it has the following three manifest characteristics: "it appears to be well made," "it has a hole of the proper shape and size at the proper location," and "it is not obviously scratched." If we define predicate c as "has the phonograph record characteristics given in the preceding sentence," then manifest predicate c can be taken to be an index of P. So if *y* satisfies c, we should infer that *y* is playable. Or, instead of c we might accept manifest predicate w, "is warranted by a reputable manufacturer of phonograph records," as an index of P. Thus, there might be a multiplicity of indexes of a given dispositional predicate (each of which is itself a manifest predicate).

Index (x,P) could then be read "phonograph record *x* satisfies an index of playability." The grounds for this reading could be the fact that phonograph record *x* has the manifest predicate c, or the fact that phonograph record *x* has the manifest predicate w, or any other manifest predicate that is taken by the scientist to be an index of dispositional predicate P. The role of P6 in the system, then, is to permit projections[2] from manifest predicates to dispositional predicates where such are required.

Of these six primitives there is one term that enables the system to deal with more than social physics (i.e., with more than an account of physical properties of social individuals and institutions). This term is P5, *individuals that have* F *believe that p.* P5 enables us to construct definitions of concepts involving notions such as *goal, purpose, intention, knowledge* (including self-knowledge), *expectation,* etc. The other five primitives are more concerned with physical or logical matters than with mental states.

With these six predicates constructed along nominalist lines, we are able to proceed with the construction of definitions, taken up in the next several chapters.

2. Nelson Goodman deals at length with the matter of projection, and the term is used here in the Goodmanian sense. He raises the issue in a discussion of the problem of dispositions: "The problem of explaining how a given manifest predicate, say 'P,' must be related to others if the fact that these others apply to a thing is to be ground for applying to that thing a broader correlative of 'P' . . ." [24: 57].

3

Auxiliary Definitions

THE first forty definitions developed from the set of primitives are called *auxiliary definitions,* which define *auxiliary terms.* Such terms have their primary significance not in their own right but insofar as they are useful modules in constructing definitions of additional terms that are important in themselves. In the same way, a jig or a mold has no direct significance as part of the final machine that is being built but does make it much easier to produce pieces of the same size and shape, or pieces that differ in some ways but contain identical parts.

Consider, for example, the ninth auxiliary definition. From primitives, previously defined terms, and several pieces of logical apparatus, we develop a new concept, the *interval-part.* An interval-part of a given thing for a given span (or interval) of time is simply the more limited object that is that-thing-during-that-time. For example, the interval-part of Thomas Jefferson for the year 1814 is (roughly) Jefferson-as-a-seventy-one-year-old, who does not write the Declaration of Independence nor serve as president of the United States but does reside at Monticello and is president of the American Philosophical Society. The notion of interval-part will be used many times in the course of constructing substantive definitions of terms that do enjoy currency, and by developing a simple label for a more complex structure we spare ourselves much burdensome repetitive construction later on. So it is with auxiliary terms in general.

Keeping in mind the merely systematic function of auxiliaries, we turn to an explication of these terms. At this point we begin to present definitions. Each definition consists of two parts: the *definiendum* (the term being defined) enclosed in quotation marks and followed by the symbol "= df." and the *definiens* (the definition) in informal form, also enclosed in quotation marks.

AUX 1   "x is part of y" = df.

"everything that overlaps x overlaps y"

This definition simply states that an individual x is a part of another individual y if any individual that has some part in common with x also has some part in common with y. Since we include any individual sharing some part of x, this means that any part of x may be involved. Thus, any part of x is a part of y, or all parts of x are part of y. A person's arm is a part of that person, since anything that has a part in common with the arm (e.g., hand, finger, skeleton, etc.) also has something in common with the person. However, it is important to note that we are speaking of things having *parts* in common with other things, not of things having *attributes* in common with other things. If we were to construct the class of all arms that have the same circumference at the elbow, we might be inclined to say that two members of that class have something in common. To be sure, all members of the class have a common attribute, but they have no part in common.

AUX 2   "x is identical to y" = df.

"x is part of y *and* y is part of x"

This term establishes *identity* between two individuals by noting that if the "part of" relation applies in both directions between any two individuals, then there can be no part of either that is not part of the other. Therefore, the two have exactly the same parts, that is, they are identical.

AUX 3   "x is a time-slice" = df.

"there is something that is an earlier time-slice than x"

This definition states that only a time-slice can bear the relation "earlier time-slice than" (introduced in P2). Therefore, if some individual is an earlier time-slice than an individual x, then x must be a time-slice. A time-slice is perhaps best visualized as a hyperplane cutting through a four-dimensional space-time continuum in such a way that every point in the hyperplane has the same value on the time axis. Thus, a time-slice is a durationless temporal cross section of the universe at a given instant, a reification of the-universe-at-a-given-moment.

AUX 4   "x is a time-interval" = df.

Conjunct 1. "every time-slice that overlaps x is part of x *and*
Conjunct 2. there are at least two distinct time-slices that are parts of
            x *and*
Conjunct 3. given any two time-slices that are parts of x, every time-
            slice later than the earlier of these *and* earlier than the
            later of them is also part of x *and*
Conjunct 4. there are time-slices earlier than any time-slice that is
            part of x *and* there are time-slices later than any time-
            slice that is part of x"

This definition constructs the notion of a *time-interval* using the following components: *time-slice, overlap, part of,* and *earlier time-slice than.* It does so in four parts, which appear in the definiens as four conjuncts, or four conditions all of which must be met. The first conjunct states that if a given time-slice overlaps the interval (has a part in common with it), then it is a part of the interval (i.e., is completely contained in it), thereby assuring that a time-interval will never contain an instant of time as a part unless it contains all simultaneous instants as well. In other words, only complete time-slices can constitute the temporal cross sections of time-intervals. The second conjunct establishes that a time-interval consists of more than one time-slice. This is a first step in ensuring that time-intervals will have temporal "thickness," that they will embrace not the-world-at-an-instant as time-slices do but the-world-over-a-period-of-time. The third conjunct provides that a time-interval has a continuous duration with no gaps or discontinuities in it. That is, a time-interval includes all the time-slices falling between its earliest time-slice (if any) and its latest one. What is not provided, here or elsewhere, is that a time-interval does actually contain a first and a last time-slice. Such intervals do have limits, both early and late, as provided by the terms of the final conjunct, but these limiting time-slices need not themselves be parts of the interval. The fourth conjunct provides that a time-interval is of finite duration. There are time-slices not in the interval that are earlier than all time-slices in the interval, and there are other time-slices not in the interval that are later than all time-slices in the interval. This does not, however, provide that an interval has a distinct beginning and a distinct ending. A given time-interval may turn out to be open or closed at either end but will always be bounded.[1]

A time-interval may perhaps best be envisaged as all that part of a four-dimensional space-time continuum that lies between two hyperplanes both of which are perpendicular to the time axis of the continuum and may be parts of the interval, external to the interval, or one of each. If a time-slice is a durationless temporal cross section of the universe, then a time-interval is a temporal cross section that has duration. If a time-slice may be said to be "tissue thin," then a time-interval has "thickness." If a time-slice is like the cut made to slice a loaf of bread, then a time-interval is like the slice of bread itself.

AUX 5   "z is the sum of x and y" = df.[2]

"w is part of z *if and only if* w is part of x *or* w is part of y"

This term defines the *sum* of two individuals as consisting of each thing that is either a part of one of the individuals or part of the other, or is partly part of one and partly part of the other without remainder. Thus, the sum of two individuals will always be that individual whose extent is just sufficient to embrace them both. Typically the sum will be more extensive than either individual alone, but this need not happen, for when y is part of x, the sum of x and y will simply be x itself. And whenever x and y are not totally discrete, their sum will be less extensive than what one would arrive at by, say, determining the volumes or the masses or the weights of x and y and then simply adding these. Sums of individuals thus construed are not normally reified as individuals in common parlance, but they sometimes are. Carolina is the sum of North Carolina and South Carolina, the Terrestrial System is the sum of Earth and its Moon, and a given baseball team's battery in a given

1. A continuous sequence of entities may or may not have a lower limit and may or may not have an upper limit. When it has a lower (upper) limit that is the largest (smallest) such limit, the limit is known as the greatest lower (least upper) bound. A particular end of a sequence is said to be closed if the sequence contains its greatest lower, or least upper, bound (whichever is at that end of the sequence). Otherwise the sequence is said to be open at that end. Obviously, a sequence can be closed at both ends, open at both ends, closed at the lower end and open at the upper, or open at the lower end and closed at the upper. Since a time-interval is a sequence of time-slices, all of this applies to time-intervals.

2. The definitions of AUX 5, 6, and 7 are nominalist versions of set operations. But because sets are forsworn, it is necessary to construct cognate operations.

game will be the sum of its pitcher and its catcher in that game. Repeated applications of this summation function can be made to build still more comprehensive entities. The construction that began with the Carolinas can culminate in Dixie, the one that began with Earth and Moon can eventually yield the Solar System, and from the baseball team's battery it is just seven more steps of summation to the team itself.

Given that we are always to count sums of individuals as individuals themselves, and that the two individuals whose sum is taken in a particular case may be contiguous parts of a single physical object (such as the part above the waist and the part below the waist of a single person) or might be quite distant and unrelated (such as Margaret Thatcher and the Alamo in San Antonio, Texas), an individual may be simple or complex. Of the entities constituted by summation in the preceding paragraph, Carolina and Dixie are simple individuals, since they are contiguous physical wholes, while the Terrestrial System, the Solar System, the baseball battery, and the baseball team are complex ones.

AUX 6   "z is the difference of x and y (x minus y)" = df.

"y is part of x *and* everything that overlaps z overlaps x *and* does not overlap y"

Here we have defined the *difference* of two individuals. The definition applies only in cases where the subtracted individual does not wholly contain the other, in other words, only in cases where z, thus defined, will exist. The definition provides that z will be that portion of x that does not overlap y. Thus, the white pieces in a chess set minus the white pawns of the same set would be the entity consisting of the white king, queen, bishops, knights, and rooks of that chess set. The white pieces minus all the pawns (black and white) would be the very same entity. And the white pieces minus all the pieces (black and white) or minus the white pieces would be undefined.

AUX 7   "z is the product of x and y" = df.

"if x overlaps y, then any w is part of z *if and only if* w is part of x, *and if* x does not overlap y, *then* z is the sum of x and y"

Here we define the *product* of two individuals as the sum of all parts common to both x and y. This predicate is defined only for the case where that sum is not null. Thus, if *y* is all the white pieces in a chess set, and *x* is all the pawns in the same chess set, the product of *x* and *y* is the white pawns of that set. Note that the product of *x* and *y* is the largest part they have in common.

AUX 8   "x is the slice-part of y in time-slice z" = df.

"z is a time-slice *and* y overlaps z *and* x is the product of y and z"

This term defines *x* as the *slice-part* of individual *y* at time *z*. That is, it defines temporal cross sections of an individual that are without thickness. We are dealing here with an individual's world-tube, also known as its space-time worm. This world-tube traces the individual's occupancy of space at all times during its existence and will, at least in any normal case, have a temporal beginning and ending (an earliest and a latest time). It is true that at a particular time the ending may not be known since that time will not have occurred yet. But this is not a matter of fact. The world-tube is always a complete entity. Starting with the notion of an individual whose career (in the sense of "extent") in space and time is its world-tube, we may thus isolate that part of the world-tube that bears any single date or time index (past, present, or future), that is, any instantaneous moment in the career of the individual. It is the concept of such an entity that is defined here. If the individual under discussion is a simple individual, then a slice-part of it is a simply connected solid with no temporal extension along its world-tube. If the individual is compound, then a slice-part of it will be a complexly connected solid. Thus, suppose that the individual is a family: mother, father, and their two adolescent children. At a particular moment mother and father are in California, while the children are visiting friends in Chicago. The slice-part of that individual at the specified time consists of four regions each of which is distinguishable from the others.

Note that for some compound individuals, there may be some date that lies within the interval spanned by the existence of the individual for which date there is no slice-part. Let us say, for example, the individual is all the kings of England. While this individual may, thus far, have spanned at least the years 1066–1950, there is no slice-part of this individual bearing the date 1600, since there was at that time no king of England; the reigning monarch in that year was Elizabeth I. Such cases fare exactly as cases in which the time chosen is before the individual came into existence in the first place or after the individual has ceased to exist. A time-slice at any such time does not overlap the individual, and hence, according to the definition, the individual has no slice-part at that time.

Summing up, then, the individual y at instant z is defined in AUX 8 as the slice-part x of y at time z, provided y has a slice-part at that time. The definition is constructed by means of three conjuncts that establish the following:

1. z is a time-slice.
2. y overlaps time-slice z; that is to say, y exists at that time.
3. x is the product of y and time-slice z.

Typically, AUX 8 will have application to what we normally think of as a physical object, the sort of thing that is capable of overlapping a time-slice so as to yield a slice-part at that time. But in spite of the highly physicalistic orientation of this study, not quite everything in the range of our variables falls into the category of physical object. Rather, that category is to be contrasted with the yet more general category of individual, which is broad enough to embrace everything whatsoever that we have allowed to fall within our domain and more besides. An individual can be mental as well as physical, abstract as well as concrete, or differ in any number of other ways from an ordinary "thing." A physical object (hereafter simply "object") is concrete and has duration and a number of other familiar characteristics common to such things. It is beyond the purposes of this study to define "object" formally in terms of our primitives, not that this could not be accomplished more or less straightforwardly. Rather, in cases where objects constitute the applications of some predicate, we will merely make certain that we do not formally introduce any limitations inconsistent with such applications. The definition of AUX 8 is clearly consistent with the stipulation that an individual must have duration. That is, an instantaneous cross section of an object is not the object but rather the object *at that instant only.* The entire object is the sum of all of its slice-parts. And, of course, both the object and its slice-parts are *individuals,* as is everything over which we allow our variables to range.

AUX 9   "x is the interval-part of y in time-interval τ" = df.

"τ is a time-interval *and* y overlaps τ *and* x is the product of y and τ"

AUX 9 defines the *interval-part* of an individual in a time-interval. This is essentially a temporally compact collection of slice-parts of that individual.

Indeed, the definition could be so constructed, but we take advantage of the earlier definition of time-interval (AUX 4) to complete the construction in simpler fashion.

AUX 10   "x and y are discrete slice-parts of z" = df.

"x is the slice-part of z in some time-slice *and* y is the slice-part of z in some different (distinct) time-slice"

AUX 11   "x is an earlier-and-discrete time-interval relative to y" = df.

"x and y are both time-intervals *and* every time-slice that is part of x is earlier than any time-slice that is part of y"

Temporal priority between time-slices is a primitive of this definitional system. Here we define *temporal priority between time-intervals.* There are three possible cases, only the first of which is covered by this definition: two nonoverlapping intervals; two overlapping intervals neither of which is a proper part of (i.e., is completely contained in) the other; and one interval is a proper part of the other and the two either begin simultaneously or end simultaneously. (In the case where one interval is a proper part of the other but they neither begin nor end simultaneously, the notion of "earlier interval than" or "later interval than" has no application.) In the first case, the interval that, in its entirety, precedes the other is unequivocally the earlier. In the second case, the interval that begins earlier and ends earlier than the other is more reasonably spoken of as the earlier interval. In the third case, the interval that begins earlier and ends simultaneously with the other, or that begins simultaneously with the other and ends earlier, is commonly thought of as the earlier. The sense of *earlier,* as defined in AUX 11, is obviously "the first."

AUX 12   "x and y are discrete interval-parts of z" = df.

"there are two time-intervals, τ and τ', that are discrete from one another, *and* x is the interval-part of z in one of them *and* y is the interval-part of z in the other"

Somewhat analogously to AUX 10, we here define the notion of *discrete interval-parts* of an individual. That is, *x* and *y,* which are interval-parts of individual *z,* are discrete interval-parts if they are parts of discrete time-intervals. Since the concept of discrete intervals has already been defined (in

AUX 11), the concept of discrete interval-parts falls immediately into place in terms of it.

> AUX 13   "τ' is a terminating time of time-interval τ" = df.
>
>> "τ is an earlier-and-discrete time-interval relative to τ' *and* there is no time-interval τ'' such that τ'' is an earlier-and-discrete time-interval relative to τ' *and* τ is an earlier-and-discrete time-interval relative to τ''"

This definition is a notational convenience for identifying a time-interval that is just later than, but not overlapping, any given time-interval. In application, such a terminating time will be short, the period just following the time-interval it terminates.

> AUX 14   "x is the fusion of the predicate '$\mathbf{F}$' " = df.
>
>> "everything that satisfies $\mathbf{F}$ is part of x, *and* everything that is part of x overlaps something that satisfies $\mathbf{F}$"

Here we define the *fusion of a predicate*. A *predicate* is a term of a language that applies to all things that have a certain attribute or relation to all the *n*-ads that stand in a certain *n*-place relation.[3] The fusion of a predicate consists of the sum of all those individuals to which the predicate applies and bears great resemblance to the notion of *class,* which is central to set theory and Platonist logic. The fusion of a predicate consists of all individuals satisfying the predicate, as the class has as its members all of the individuals that have the class attribute. It is not, however, as straightforward a matter to retrieve the predicate from its fusion as it is to retrieve a class attribute from the class. A given thing has the attribute just in case it is a member of the class, but a thing's satisfying the predicate is no simple matter of its being a part of the fusion. Where a person is any member of the class of persons, most parts of the fusion of persons will not be persons but will be parts of persons, or things that have persons as parts, or still more irregular entities that overlap two or more different persons.

Though one might regard this difficulty as a shortcoming of the nominalistic approach, it may also be seen as a virtue. Having to isolate the special parts of a fusion that satisfy its predicate necessitates greater articulation on our part. It promotes clarity to have to specify, for example, just what it is

---

3. An *n*-ad is a collection of objects. An *n*-place relation is a relation among objects (e.g., in "*x* is father of *y*," *father of* is an *n*-place relation).

that distinguishes persons from less integrally constituted entities made up of the same components. Such obligatory clarity would become especially important when, as in later stages of this line of activity,[4] predicates such as "organization" might be in question. Applications of these predicates depend relatively little on the constituents of the things they apply to but rely heavily on delicate features of the relations in which those constituents stand to one another.

AUX 15   "x satisfies an index of **F** in time-interval τ" = df.

"the interval-part of x in time-interval τ satisfies an index of **F**"

Here we have defined the *satisfaction of an index* by individual x during a time-interval τ. This is done by applying the predicate schema of P6 to the interval-part, in time-interval τ, of x where x is an individual whose world-tube passes through time-interval τ. Thus, if a piece of paper is immersed in water throughout a time-interval, say from August 10, 1982, through November 15, 1982, then it would not satisfy the index "combustible" during that interval. However, during the interval following the removal of the paper from the water, assuming that it is then dried and stays in an oxygen-rich atmosphere, it would then satisfy the index.

AUX 16   "on the grounds that he is an **F**, x believes, in time-interval τ, that p" = df.

"individuals that have **F** believe that p, *and* the interval-part of x in time-interval τ is an **F**"

AUX 16 defines the notion of *overt belief* by an individual x in time-interval τ. The appropriately chosen predicate for use with P5 can be ascribed to an individual satisfying the predicate of belief in p. Overt belief occurs when the predicate chosen is manifested by x at time τ, provided that those who satisfy that predicate believe p. Thus, let F mean "persons who genuflect before the altar upon entering a Roman Catholic church" and "p" mean "the pope is infallible." We can now define AUX 16, "on the grounds that he is a person who genuflects before the altar upon entering a Roman Catholic church, x believes, in time-interval τ, that the pope is infallible," as follows: "Persons who genuflect before the altar when entering a Roman Catholic

4. Not pursued in this volume but to be taken up in subsequent work.

church believe that the pope is infallible, and the individual who is x at time τ genuflects before the altar upon entering a Roman Catholic church."

AUX 17   "on the grounds that he is **F**-able, x believes, in time-interval τ, that p" = df.

"on the grounds that he is an **F**, x believes, in time-interval τ, that p; *or* individuals that have **F** believe that p *and* the interval-part of x in time-interval τ satisfies an index of **F**"

AUX 16 is here extended to cover not only the original case of the individual who, during interval τ, displays F (genuflects before the altar upon entering a Roman Catholic church) but also the case of the individual who does not display F (perhaps because he has not entered a Roman Catholic church during that interval) but of whom it is known, by virtue of such other behavior as membership in the Knights of Columbus or deferential manner in the presence of Roman Catholic clergy, that he would display F if the proper conditions were met (e.g., if he entered a Roman Catholic church). Such a person, by his F-ness or his F-ability, gives a basis for our adducing his belief in *p*.

AUX 18   "x believes, in time-interval τ, that p" = df.

"there is at least one predicate **F** such that on the grounds that x is **F**-able, x believes, in time-interval τ, that p"

Here we define *belief by x in τ that p*, adduced by the observer on whatever basis. Again, let *p* mean "the pope is infallible." AUX 18 states that there is at least one predicate F in our language such that on the grounds that *x* satisfies F or an index of F, *x* believes, in time-interval τ, that the pope is infallible. Predicate F may be one of the following:

genuflects before the altar when he enters a Roman Catholic church;
has a plastic image of Christ on the dashboard of his automobile;
is frequently heard to say "Jesus, Mary, and Joseph" instead of "goddamn" or other common blasphemies;
is a member of the Knights of Columbus;
invariably refers to the pope as "the Holy Father."

AUX 19   "x has veridical belief, in time-interval τ, that p" = df.

" 'p' is true *and* x believes, in time-interval τ, that p"

If p is a true statement and individual x believes p in time-interval τ, then we say that x has veridical (i.e., true or correct) belief, in τ, that p is true.

AUX 20   "x has nonveridical belief, in time-interval τ, that p" = df.

   " 'p' is false *and* x believes, in time-interval τ, that p"

AUX 21   "x perceives, in time-interval τ, that p" = df.

   "x believes, in time-interval τ, that p"

Note that because perception is identified with belief, AUX 21 is identical to AUX 18.

AUX 22   "x veridically perceives, in time-interval τ, that p" = df.

   "x has veridical belief, in time-interval τ, that p"

Again, because of the identity of perception and belief, AUX 22 is identical to AUX 19.

AUX 23   "x nonveridically perceives, in time-interval τ, that p"
   = df.

   "x has nonveridical belief, in time-interval τ, that p"

Note that AUX 23 is identical to AUX 20.

In AUX 21–23 perception is identified with belief, while AUX 18–20 draw veridical/nonveridical distinctions. It is helpful to clarify just what we mean by "veridical perception," and there are two questions to face in this regard. First, do we have access to objective reality? Second, is some perception of that reality an objective, or veridical, perception? The first question must always be answered in the affirmative as long as we have some sort of functioning sensory apparatus. It is with respect to the second question that AUX 22 and AUX 23 draw distinctions.

AUX 24   "**F** is a universal predicate" = df.

   "for all x, x is an **F**"

A predicate F is a *universal predicate* if it is satisfied by all individuals. That is, a universal predicate is a descriptor that is true of every individual (e.g., if F were "is an individual," then F would be a universal predicate).

AUX 25   "**F** is a one-place morphological predicate" = df.

"**F** is not a universal predicate *and* whenever two things are morphologically identical one is an **F** *if and only if* the other is also"

A predicate F is a *one-place morphological predicate* if it is not a universal predicate (i.e., if there are individuals that do not satisfy it) and if two morphologically identical individuals both satisfy F or both fail to satisfy F. In AUX 25, F is a one-place predicate as indicated by the expression "*x* is an F," as opposed to such expressions as "bears F to," which characterize relational predicates of two or more places.

AUX 26   "x undergoes change with respect to predicate **F** in time-interval τ" = df.

"τ is a time-interval *and* there are two time-intervals y and z that are parts of τ such that the interval-part of x with respect to one of them is an **F** *and* the interval-part of x with respect to the other is not"

According to AUX 26, *x undergoes change with respect to predicate* F in time-interval τ if in that interval *x* is at one time an F and at some other time is not. Thus, if Mr. Smith is employed for the summer of 1983, but during the fall of that year he is unemployed, then he has undergone change with respect to his employment (F) during that year.

AUX 27   "x undergoes morphological change with respect to predicate **F** in time-interval τ" = df.

"**F** is a one-place morphological predicate *and* x undergoes change with respect to predicate **F** in time-interval τ"

AUX 28   "x undergoes change in time-interval τ" = df.

"there is at least one predicate **F** in the language such that **F**-change has occurred with respect to that predicate in time-interval τ"

This generalizes AUX 26 over predicates.

AUX 29   "x undergoes morphological change in time-interval τ"
= df.

> "x undergoes morphological change with respect to some one-place morphological predicate in time-interval τ"

AUX 30   "**K** is a behavioral predicate" = df.

> "whenever anything satisfies **K** there is a time when it does so *and* satisfies some predicate **F** that it does not satisfy at some other time when it satisfies **K**"

By this definition, κ is a *behavioral predicate* if any individual that satisfies κ in a given time-interval undergoes change with respect to some predicate in that interval. That is, if all individuals that satisfy κ in time-interval τ also changes in τ, then κ is a behavioral predicate. For example, if κ is "catches the ball," then an individual to whom this applies over a given period will satisfy "holds the ball" at some time during that period but will not satisfy it at some other time during the period.

AUX 31   "x exhibits **K**-behavior in time-interval τ" = df.

> "**K** is a behavioral predicate *and* τ is a time-interval *and* the interval-part of x in τ is a **K**"

To exhibit κ-behavior at a given time is simply to be a κ at that time, where κ is a behavioral predicate. To exhibit ball-catching behavior during the warm-up period is nothing more nor less than to catch a ball during the warm-up period.

AUX 32   "x exhibits behavior in time-interval τ" = df.

> "x exhibits **K**-behavior in time-interval τ with respect to some behavioral predicate **K**"

This definition is an extension of AUX 31 to cover the general case. That is, with respect to any predicate at all (just so long as it is in the language), say Q, if *x* exhibits Q-behavior, then *x* exhibits behavior.

AUX 33   "**K** is a behavioral predicate with respect to **F**-change"
= df.

> "all and only those things that satisfy **K** during a given time-interval undergo **F**-change during that time-interval"

This is a specification of AUX 31, identifying the particular type of change by virtue of which κ is behavioral. Thus, "sits down" is a behavioral predicate with respect to change in satisfaction of some appropriate physical-posture predicate such as "is in a sitting position."

AUX 34   "x exhibits morphological **K**-behavior in time-interval τ"
             = df.

             "for some morphological predicate **F**, **K** is a behavioral predicate with respect to **F**-change *and* x exhibits **K**-behavior in time-interval τ"

AUX 35   "x exhibits morphological behavior in time-interval τ"
             = df.

             "for some predicate **K**, x exhibits morphological **K**-behavior in time-interval τ"

AUX 36   "x is an event at time τ" = df.

             "some part of x behaves in time-interval τ"

AUX 37   "x is an event" = df.

             "for some time-interval τ, x is an event at time τ"

Thus, an *event* is any piece of reality at least some part of which undergoes change. Only something entirely static would fail to qualify as an event. Thus, moving one's hand is an event, but remaining seated and in no way changing is not an event. There is one respect in which this definition does not agree with common usage. An event is usually associated with a moment in time, whereas here we refer to an interval. We can justify this by pointing out that a moment in time is literally not observable, and an event should be. Clearly, though, the interval in question should not be very long.

The next set of definitions (AUX 38–40) is concerned with future-oriented concepts. *Expectations* are beliefs about the future. *Plans* deal with intentions regarding future actions of the agent. Plans occur in situations in which an actor x believes, at time τ' earlier-and-discrete relative to τ, that at time τ x will behave in a given fashion. Actor x has expectations when x believes, at time τ', earlier-and-discrete relative to τ, that at time τ some event will occur. A plan seems to be a special case of an expectation, that is, if the event that is expected to occur is the behavior of the actor x itself, then the expectation is a plan. Note that this deviates slightly from the colloquial conception of plan in that a plan is usually conceived of as an intended behavior, while this definition includes an action that an actor expects to take, even though he neither desires nor intends to take it. For example, suppose x is a prisoner of the Chilean junta. He believes, on Monday morning at ten o'clock, that at two o'clock that afternoon he will be taken from his cell for interrogation and that after he has been tortured for some time he will implicate others in his anti-junta activities. He neither intends nor desires to do that, but he expects that he will, and we allow this to count as a plan.

Thus, behavior under physical, psychological, or chemical duress would qualify as a plan if it is behavior that the agent expects he will take, even though he may not desire to take it. Some would say that this sort of unintended change is neither behavior nor action, but it is consistent with our definition of behavior (cf. definitions AUX 30 et. seq.) and with our preference for objective measures rather than relying on unobservable internal states.

AUX 38   "person x expects, in time-interval τ, that event y will occur in time-interval τ'" = df.

"x believes, in time-interval τ, that y is an event that occurs in time-interval τ', *and* τ is an earlier-and-discrete time-interval relative to τ'"

AUX 39   "person x plans, in time-interval τ, that x exhibits **B**-behavior in time-interval τ'" = df.

"x believes, in time-interval τ, that x exhibits **B**-behavior in time-interval τ', *and* τ is an earlier-and-discrete time-interval relative to τ'"

In this definition, в refers to any sort of behavioral predicate (as in AUX 30 and 31). Any of the terms defined earlier in this chapter, as well as many of those defined in chapter 4, could occur here.

AUX 40   "persons x and y mutually plan, in time-interval τ, that x will exhibit **B**-behavior in time-interval τ' *and* y will exhibit **B**'-behavior in time-interval τ''" = df.

"person x plans, in time-interval τ, that x will exhibit **B**-behavior in time-interval τ', *and* person x expects, in time-

> interval τ, that person y will exhibit **B**'-behavior in time-interval τ'', *and* person y plans, in time-interval τ, that y will exhibit **B**'-behavior in time-interval τ'', *and* person y expects, in time-interval τ, that person x will exhibit **B**-behavior in time-interval τ'''

A *mutual plan* occurs when two or more persons have mutually consistent plans about their own behavior as well as mutually consistent expectations about each other's behavior at some future time or times. That is, each person plans some behavior that is expected by the other or others, and each expects some behavior of the other or others that is planned by them, at consistent times. Of course, these plans and expectations can involve all sorts of behavior.

We have now completed the definition of the auxiliary terms. Although many of these terms are of little interest in isolation, they do work in systematic cooperation with one another and will facilitate the defining of more meaningful terms. In the next two chapters we construct definitions in two content areas: psychology and sociology.

4

Decision and Purposive Behavior

Decision and Behavior

Decision and *choice* are inextricably involved with one another in human thought and life. The two terms are descriptive of two slightly different ways of looking at the complex process that begins with the assessment or appraisal of possibilities, moves through the weighing of conditions and alternatives, and ends with the actual commitment of resources and self to a course of action. Decision analysis precedes the making of choice. To decide is a mental action. To choose is to prepare to begin the physical action that, when carried to completion, and whether successful or not in the attainment of desired ends, represents the implementation of the decision. This action, which is the major observable in the process, will be called decision behavior or purposive behavior.

Decision and choice are almost as inseparable as two parts of walking: raising the foot and placing it back upon the ground. Decision without choice means that no action takes place. Choice without decision means that the choice was unplanned, or entirely reactive.

Decision and decision behavior must be distinguished from whatever it is that leads to the spasmodic, undeliberated, or unchosen action. The fact of a decision can only be inferred by an outside observer. This inference is based upon actions that the putative actor-cum-decision-maker carries out and can be further supported by claims made by the decision maker. If, however, the claims are unaccompanied by action, there are problems in sorting out pure fancy from real, albeit ineffectual, decision.

Certain types of action supply the basis for inferring nondecision as the antecedent mental state. The responses of reflex arcs, as when certain points on the body are struck, are clearly classifiable as nondecision behavior. The cry of pain, the counterproductive action sometimes taken under stress, is another candidate for classification as nondecision behavior.

But *deliberate* actions (i.e., those not taken under great short-term stress nor impelled by biomechanical response patterns of the human organism) are more likely to have been preceded by decision. It is this sort of behavior and its mental antecedents with which we are concerned here.

Decisions can be classified according to many schemes. Some categories of decision lend themselves to detailed analysis, and others do not. But whether or not a particular category of decision is, or is believed to be, capable of being analyzed, one important matter must not be lost sight of: Decision making is part of the behavior of human beings (and of other purposeful creatures, if any), and therefore all decisions should be recognized as being of equal concern to students of human behavior. The way in which this concern can be expressed depends, of course, on the investigator's belief about what can be done with this or that category of decision. If the category is believed to be subject to analysis, then that enterprise should be carried forward. If the category resists analysis, then any of the various means available to scientific investigators should be used to identify and isolate the unanalyzable while taking account of its effect on analyzable substance to the greatest extent possible. An example of this process is the carrying of an error term in a behavior equation of an econometric model. The error term generally takes into account two sorts of elements: (1) those factors of the study that, for whatever reason, are not subject to analysis, and (2) errors of observation or measurement.

Moreover, the fact that a decision is believed to be "irrational" is no basis for denying it as a datum of human behavior. That this is frequently the way in which "nonrational" or "irrational" decisions are handled is poor scientific practice. Indeed, the question of what is meant by "rational" varies from investigator to investigator. And the use of the terms "nonrational" and "irrational" as the complement of "rational," however defined, has pejorative connotations outside the tradition of proper scientific investigation. Finally, classification of a decision as "nonrational" or "irrational" does not deny the possibility of analysis. A key aspect of the scientific endeavor is an awareness of the method's own incompleteness and shortcomings, and we do well to recognize the study of the unanalyzed decision as work to be completed some day in the future, perhaps with other tools by other investigators, not to say other kinds of investigators.

Investigators interested in decision behavior represent a broad range of disciplines, including psychology, economics, sociology, social anthropology, political science, mathematics, philosophy, and psychiatry.[1] Indeed, issues of what a decision is and how decision behavior can be observed, measured, classified, analyzed, and predicted have been a central concern of the investigators of human behavior for as long as there have been efforts made to analyze and understand human motivation and behavior. The concern with decision behavior has been of both an analytic and a prescriptive nature and has been expressed throughout history in philosophy, in literature (for examples of prescriptive concern with decisions, see Polonius's advice to Laertes in *Hamlet,* Act III, Scene I, and Chesterfield's *Letters to His Son*), in political and religious tracts, in works on ethics, and in recent analytical works. The result has been widespread agreement on the identification of at least some of the central elements of decision behavior.[2] Our classification of these elements will not be substantially different from those in general use, although it is hoped that it will be more inclusive and less parochial than most individual discussions of decision behavior.

A decision, as distinguished from the mental state characterized by the absence of decision, and as an antecedent to choice, is understood to be associated with purposive, or goal-seeking, behavior. That is, associated with a decision there must be some object, some state of affairs, that is sought and that is valued more highly than some other states of affairs. A decision is a commitment to action that is calculated to increase the likelihood of achieving one or more such states of affairs. Consequently, decision making involves some conception of possible future states of affairs and of the processes whereby these future states are *believed* to be brought into actuality. Without an understanding of the future as a subset of the not-as-yet-actualized, the entire notion of purposive behavior becomes empty. And purposive behavior is absolutely required in order for a decision to have any meaning. Moreover, for present action and future state to be meaningfully connected in the mind of the decision maker, there must be some belief, erroneous or not, about the nature of sociophysical evolutionary processes that result in the generation of future states of affairs out of the present state of affairs and actions taken in the present.

In addition there must be some means of *evaluating* future states of affairs.

1. As just one example, the list of participants in the seminar on the Design of Experiments in Decision Processes, held in Santa Monica, California, in the summer of 1952, reveals the following disciplinary distribution: eight economists, eight psychologists, eleven mathematicians, five philosophers, two statisticians, one sociologist, two political scientists, and two systems analysts [67: 329, 331].

2. See, for example, [39: 12].

It must be possible to speak of the relative desirabilities of these states and to establish measurement scales for them. And that is precisely what we are concerned with here. There are, of course, many schemes for constructing measurement scales; they range from the simplest sort of classification scheme (by color, for example, or of foods by taste: salty, sweet, sour, bitter, etc.) through a variety of partial and complete orderings, ordered metrics, interval scales, and cardinal measure scales [66], [12]. As we move toward the end of this listing, we open up the possibility of more and more exactitude and mathematical power being available to us. That is, insofar as it is legitimate to claim that cardinal measure is possible, to that degree the full power of mathematical analysis is available to us and, consequently, the more powerful are the results we may be able to achieve. But to claim cardinal measurement as a possibility and to establish it empirically are two different matters. The literature of decision theory is largely based on the a priori assumption of cardinal measurability of the values of future states. Concern with this evaluation process typically comes under such a general heading as utility theory, utility function, or payoff function. But the a priori assumption of cardinal measurability raises some treacherous questions that warrant further discussion.

Another difficulty obtrudes in this problem of establishing an appropriate measurement scale, one that is frequently assumed away. This has to do with the possibility of combining disparate aspects of a future state of affairs, or, for our purposes, of evaluating these disparate aspects on a common scale. It is conceivable, and indeed it has been suggested, that the valuation process may be multidimensional [9] and that the various dimensions may be mutually incommensurable. In any case some scheme must be devised that allows choices to be made among alternative states.

One such scheme might, as a complete admission of defeat in face of the difficulty, rank future states by a random drawing process. Another might involve random selection of priorities among incommensurable dimensions. Still another scheme, usually referred to as a lexicographically ordered payoff function, might assign, a priori, priorities among dimensions. Finally, weights might be assigned, by random or a priori process, to facilitate the collapse of a vector into its weighted average.

For the relative evaluation of possible future states to have meaning, there must be at least two alternative states to be compared. There must be the possibility of choice among objectives; otherwise there is no need for, nor possibility of, decision. Moreover, there must be some belief, erroneous or not, that it is possible to influence the process by which one or another of the two states comes into being. That is, there must be a meaningful (or apparently meaningful) choice to be made among actions.

Decision, choice, and action can be viewed as a process of contention against forces or obstacles that, without the action being taken, might prevent the attainment of the valued outcome. The contention may be seen as action against human competitors, rivals, or adversaries (either individuals or groups) or as action against natural (i.e., nonhuman) obstacles or forces. In this chapter we set aside the former case. That is, we assume that there are natural circumstances or forces (e.g., accidents, weather and natural occurrences, "acts of God," etc.) that may hinder the actor in his or her attempts to reach an objective (although there is no reason to rule out natural forces that help the actor). If these forces are understood sufficiently well so that their incidence, direction, and/or effects can be forecast, then it is useful to take this forecast into account. In this sense the natural occurrence can be treated as the action of an adversary carrying out a strategy (i.e., plan of action) that can be described in terms of the forecast.

Finally, in this preliminary discussion mention must be made of the support that some experimental studies have lent to the apparently nonrational attachment of decision makers to certain decision attributes. Along these lines some psychologists suggest that some individuals, despite reason for behaving otherwise, tend to prefer to act as if the choice situation is governed by certain specific probabilities of winning or losing rather than by others. In general, such attachments, which may reflect ways of reducing data-processing load and simplifying the evaluation and selection process, have been examined in constricted experimental contexts conducted largely by psychologists and social psychologists. The findings also seem to overlap studies of social perception that are concerned with the extent to which evaluative activities affect perception (e.g., the relative size appearance of coins of various values, etc.).

In this chapter a number of definitions are developed that focus on the notion of purposive behavior. This concept is identified with decision behavior. In order to develop the notion of purpose, an apparatus is first constructed that centers on the idea of function.

Functionality

With the DEC (decision) terms we leave the realm of pure apparatus and begin constructing definitions of terms that have recognizable human and social content. At first, this feature of recognizability will be somewhat faint and will be more true of definienda (terms being defined) than of definientia (the definitional structures themselves). But as the pool of recognizable definienda grows, definientia in which they are incorporated will begin to make more intuitive sense.

In constructing the DEC definitions I am concerned with the behaviors of individuals. My ultimate concern in the development of this group of terms is the ability to speak logically and meaningfully of purpose and decision. I begin by developing the notion of a *functional predicate*. In this context, functionality is a property of a predicate that might be conceived of as a descriptor of a set of predicates.

Consider the predicate "uses, at time τ, a means of urban transit." There are various means of urban transit, and there are other means of transit that are not used within urban settings. Thus, motorbuses, light- and heavy-rail rapid transit (above, at, or below ground level), private automobiles, taxicabs, motorcycles and motorbikes, bicycles, roller skates, and helicopters are all means of urban transit; that is, they are all suitable ways of traveling from one point to another within a densely settled and heavily traveled city. But fixed-wing aircraft, long-distance motorcoach, long-distance rail, and transoceanic ship are means of transport that are unsuitable for urban settings. So the predicate "uses, at time τ, a means of urban transit" is a predicate had by each individual using, at time τ, any means of urban transport (i.e., using any of the above-listed means of transport suitable for use within an urban setting). And each individual using, at time τ, the vehicle named New York Metropolitan Transit Authority motorbus no. 3751, or Central New York Regional Transit Organization motorbus no. 235, or any other specific motorbus has the predicate "uses, at time τ, an urban bus." Similarly, each individual who uses, at time τ, an identifiable unit of urban transit, be it automobile, rail rapid transit, motorbike or motorcycle, bicycle, and so on, has an associated predicate: "uses, at time τ, an auto," "uses, at time τ, rail rapid transit," etc. Moreover, by virtue of the definition of "uses, at time τ, a means of urban transit," every individual that has one of the predicates previously alluded to also has the predicate "uses, at time τ, a means of urban transit." In other words, everything in the fusion of "uses, at time τ, a bicycle" (i.e., all the individuals that have "uses, at time τ, a bicycle" and all the individuals that overlap individuals that have "uses, at time τ, a bicycle") and everything in the fusion of each predicate of the form "uses, at time τ, a Z" (where in place of Z we put the name of some means of urban transit) will have the predicate "uses, at time τ, a means of urban transit." Finally, an individual that has any of those above-listed predicates is conduced to have the predicate "is transported within the city." Since it is not possible, at a given time, to use more than one means of urban transit, the fusion of any of these predicates that refers to a specific form of urban transit is disjoint from the fusion of each other such predicate. We would say in this case that "uses, at time τ, a means of urban transit" is a functional predicate.

A *functional predicate,* then, is a predicate that describes a class of predicates whose fusions are disjoint and each of which has the same general sort of consequence for the individual that has any of that class of predicates. In the example just given, each predicate, if it is had by an individual, conduces that the individual be transported within the city at a given time.

Listed below are examples of functional predicates along with their component predicates and the objective predicates that individual b is conduced to have when individual x, the agent, has at least one of the component predicates:

Example 1.
(**K**):Enters the house at time τ, carrying parcel b
   (**F**1):Enters the house via the front door at time τ
   (**F**2):Enters the house via the rear door at time τ
   (**F**3):Enters the house via the bedroom window at time τ
   (**F**4):Enters the house via the basement window at time τ
   (**F**5):et cetera
      (**H**[a]):Parcel b is placed on the living room table at time τ

Example 2.
(**K**):Cleans red-striped necktie at time τ
   (**F**1):Cleans red-striped necktie with soap at time τ
   (**F**2):Cleans red-striped necktie with detergent at time τ
   (**F**3):Sends red-striped necktie to cleaner at time τ
   (**F**4):et cetera
      (**H**[a]):Soup stain is removed from red-striped necktie b at time τ

Example 3.
(**K**):Performs appendectomy on patient b at time τ
   (**F**1):Makes McBurney incision on patient b and performs appendectomy at time τ
   (**F**2):Makes lateral abdominal incision on patient b and performs appendectomy at time τ

(**F**3):Makes cranial incision on patient *b* and performs appendectomy at time τ

(**F**4):Makes dorsal incision on patient *b* and performs appendectomy at time τ

(**F**5):et cetera

(**H**[a]):Patient *b* is free of risk of appendicitis from time τ onward

Example 4.

(**K**):Studies calculus at time τ

(**F**1):Takes Math 215 from Professor I. Newton at time τ

(**F**2):Takes Math 215 from Professor G. W. Leibniz at time τ

(**F**3):Studies calculus using a self-paced, programmed instruction text for Math 215 at time τ

(**F**4):et cetera

(**H**[a]):Student *b* learns calculus at time τ

Example 5.

(**K**):Runs for president of the United States at time τ

(**F**1):Runs for president of the United States as Democratic party candidate at time τ

(**F**2):Runs for president of the United States as Republican party candidate at time τ

(**F**3):Runs for president of the United States as candidate of a minor political party at time τ

(**F**4):Runs for president of the United States as independent candidate at time τ

(**H**[a]):Individual *b* is elected president of the United States at time τ

Note that individual *x,* the agent, and individual *b,* the individual that is conduced as a consequence to have the objective predicate, may be the same individual (as in the last two examples) or distinct individuals (as in the first three examples). To summarize, κ is a functional predicate if there are at least two predicates (ϝ and ɢ) only one of which may be displayed by an agent at a time and each of which is conducive to individual *b* having another predicate (ʜ).

The Definitions

DEC 1   "**K** is an (**FG**)-for-**H**[b] functional predicate" = df.

"for all x, *if* x has **F**, *or if* x has **G**, *then* x has **K** *and* **F** is a morphological predicate *and* **G** is a morphological predicate *and* the y that is the fusion of **F** is disjunct from the z that is the fusion of **G** *and* the fusion of **F** conduces that b will have **H** *and* the fusion of **G** conduces that b will have **H**"

A functional predicate is a labeled predicate. What I am interested in labeling here is behavior. *Functional behavior* is behavior that has a functional predicate. Thus, κ is a behavioral predicate (i.e., if an individual has κ then it undergoes change) and it is a functional predicate.

DEC 2   "x exhibits **K**(**FG**)-for-**H**[b] functional behavior in time-interval τ" = df.

"**K** is an (**FG**)-for-**H**[b] functional predicate *and* the y that is the interval-part of x in time-interval τ has **F** *or* the y that is the interval-part of x in time-interval τ has **G** *and* **K** is a behavioral predicate"

This definition defines particular functional behavior with respect to a functional predicate. That is, *x* has κ (e.g., makes an abdominal incision on patient *b* at time τ) by virtue of having F or G, and this behavior of type κ conduces that *b* will have H (will be free of risk from appendicitis at time τ). Suppose that *x* has κ by virtue of some unspecified F or G and that the fusions of this F and this G separately conduce to *b* having some unspecified H. In that case κ is a functional predicate associated with some unspecified F, G, and H, where individual *b* is the specific individual that has whichever H is associated with the predicate κ, and κ is a *b*-oriented functional predicate.

DEC 3   "**K** is a b-oriented functional predicate" = df.

"**K** is a functional predicate that is (**FG**)-for-**H**[b], for some **F**, **G**, and **H**"

DEC 4 rings the same changes on DEC 3 as were rung on DEC 1 in deriving DEC 2.

DEC 4   "x exhibits b-oriented functional **K**-behavior in time-interval τ" = df.

"x exhibits functional **K(FG)**-for-**H**[b] behavior in time-interval τ, for some **F**, **G**, and **H**"

DEC 5 generalizes DEC 4 with respect to some (unspecified) K.

DEC 5   "x exhibits b-oriented functional behavior" = df.

"x exhibits b-oriented functional **K**-behavior in time-interval τ, for some **K**"

DEC 6 generalizes DEC 5 with respect to *b*.

DEC 6   "x exhibits functional behavior in time-interval τ" = df.

"for some y, x exhibits y-oriented functional behavior in time-interval τ"

Purposive behavior is the proclivity to carry out one or more of a class of behaviors, each different from the others but each of which would result in the attainment of the same, or very similar, states of affairs. Thus, an agent (i.e., an actor) may display purposive behavior with respect to some goal states but not to others. We speak of someone displaying K(FG)-for-H[b] purposive behavior, where F and G are predicates referring to different sorts of action both of which belong to the class K of actions, any member of which will eventuate in a certain type of state of affairs. So, K may be the class of actions involving transporting a person a few miles through traffic in an urban environment. An individual may be a K(FG)-for-H[b] purposive behaver, where " K(FG)-for-H[b]" refers to the selection on a morning of one (F or G) of a number of means of urban transit (K). The agent might ride in his own car or in a friend's car, or ride a bus or a bicycle, etc., in order to get himself (*b*) to his office on time (H). But the same individual may not be an L(MN)-for-J[b] purposive behaver, where L is the class of actions, such as M and N, that are involved in cooking breakfast so that the agent could get a warm breakfast (J[b]). In this case, rather than doing L(MN)-for-J[b], he munches mechanically, randomly, and absent-mindedly on whatever he encounters upon reaching into boxes in his pantry while reading the morning paper. That is, the morning paper, not his breakfast, has his purposive attention. Built into this concept of purposive behavior, then, is the respect or respects in which one counts as a purposive behaver.

Purposive behavior cannot be viewed simply as action that leads to a specified state of affairs. Any simple automaton exhibits that kind of action. Neither would we characterize the action of a thermostatic furnace, a refrigerator control, or a toilet-flush mechanism as purposive or decision-making behavior. Rather, to display purposive behavior is to act in a way that is expected to result in the attainment of a specified state of affairs while alternative means to the attainment of the same state are available and known to the actor. Moreover, we should be able to infer (in ways that are set out as observational techniques are developed) that if conditions are unfavorable and one strategy fails, one or more of the remaining alternatives will be selected in appropriate sequence, so that in most circumstances there is a greater probability of successful attainment of the goal than there would be if a smaller number of strategies were available. The use of "(FG)" should not be taken as indicative of only two strategies but as specimen members of the class K (which is possibly very large). Specifically, F and G are two predicates the behaver is known by the investigator to be disposed to satisfy in attempting to attain the goal. They constitute the investigator's evidence that the behaver satisfies K or at any rate enough of the evidence to justify the imputation of purposiveness.

A purposive behaver is not necessarily purposive about everything. In the example given above, the agent is behaving purposively about getting to the office on time but not about having a warm breakfast. He is a K(FG)-for-H[b] purposive behaver but not an L(MN)-for-J[b] purposive behaver. In addition, we do not rule out the possibility of a nonhuman animal or of a computer running under the proper program being a purposive behaver with respect to certain sorts of goals. Finally, an individual may be a K(FG)-for-H[b] purposive behaver at one time and not at another. Indeed, this is very commonly the case. In fact, perhaps much of the time a human being may not be any sort of purposive behaver whatever.

With the definitions of various levels of functional behavior in hand, it is now possible to define *overt purposive* K(FG)-for-H[b] *behavior.* The central issue in this definition is that the individual displaying overt purposive K(FG)-for-H[b] behavior must have displayed at least two of the predicates that are elements of the class of predicates comprising that functional behavior. These two behaviors must have been displayed during two discrete (nonoverlapping) time-intervals both of which are parts of the time-interval in which the overt purposive behavior has occurred. Thus, to display overt purposive K(FG)-for-H[b] behavior is at least to display a change (F) such that K is a behavioral predicate with respect to F-change, and upon finding that that change F is not followed by H[b], then to display a different change (G) such that K is a behavioral predicate with respect to G-change, given that K is an (FG)-for-H[b] functional predicate.

DEC 7   "x exhibits overt purposive **K(FG)**-for-**H**[b] behavior in time-interval τ" = df.

"for some y and y', both of which are discrete interval-parts of x in time-interval τ *and* both of which exhibit functional **K(FG)**-for-**H**[b] behavior in time-interval τ, y has **F** and not **G** *and* y' has **G** and not **F**"

Note that the fact that y and y' are discrete interval-parts of x implies that if for each we were to construct the smallest time-interval that could contain it, then each would be in a time-interval that would not overlap the time-interval in which the other is. Thus, one must be in an earlier interval than the other and therefore y is either earlier than or later than y', but they are not, even in part, simultaneous. So x has displayed F before displaying G, or x has displayed G before displaying F. And both have been displayed because the first behavior displayed has been found not to lead to b's having H. Thus, in this definition purpose is implied by pursuit of the goal H[b] by the utilization of alternative, successive means.

Purposive K(FG)-for-H[b] *behavior* is defined so as to allow the imputation of purpose in those cases in which the first behavior displayed proves successful in the attainment of the goal H[b]. Purposive K(FG)-for-H[b] behavior is defined as either the display of overt purposive K(FG)-for-H[b] behavior or, if the first behavior displayed proves successful, satisfaction of an index of overt purposive K(FG)-for-H[b] behavior. That is, if the first behavior attempted proves successful, then some evidence is found that had that not been the case another behavior of the same function would have been attempted, and so forth.

DEC 8   "x exhibits purposive **K(FG)**-for-**H**[b] behavior in time-interval τ" = df.

"x exhibits overt purposive **K(FG)**-for-**H**[b] behavior in time-interval τ *or* there is a time-interval τ' that is part of τ *and* x satisfies an index of overt purposive **K(FG)**-for-**H**[b] behavior in τ *and* (the y that is the interval-part of x in τ' has **F** and does not have **G** *or* the y that is the interval-part of x in τ' has **G** and does not have **F**)"

Purposive b-oriented behavior is any purposive behavior, involving any changes and any functional behavior, as long as whatever predicate **H** it is that becomes true of some individual becomes true of individual *b*.

DEC 9   "x exhibits purposive b-oriented behavior in time-interval
τ" = df.

"x exhibits, for some **K**, **F**, **G**, and **H**, purposive **K(FG)**-for-**H**[b] behavior in time-interval τ"

Purposive behavior is purposive *b*-oriented behavior carried out with respect to any individual *b* whatever. Thus, purposive behavior is completely general in terms of types of behavior, goal state, and the individual whose state is the object of the behavior.

DEC 10   "x exhibits purposive behavior in time-interval τ" = df.

"there is a y such that x exhibits purposive y-oriented behavior in time-interval τ"

A K(FG)-for-H[b] *psychological individual* is an individual that displays K(FG)-for-H[b] purposive behavior or that does not display K(FG)-for-H[b] functional behavior (and therefore does not display K(FG)-for-H[b] purposive behavior) but does satisfy an index of K(FG)-for-H[b] purposive behavior. That is, although the individual does not display K(FG)-for-H[b] purposive behavior, it gives the investigator reason to believe that the individual is disposed to display K(FG)-for-H[b] in some circumstances.

DEC 11   "x is a **K(FG)**-for-**H**[b] psychological individual in
time-interval τ" = df.

"x exhibits purposive **K(FG)**-for-**H**[b] behavior in time-interval τ *or* (x does not exhibit functional **K(FG)**-for-**H**[b] behavior in time-interval τ *and* x satisfies an index of purposive **K(FG)**-for-**H**[b] behavior in time-interval τ)"

A *psychological individual* in time-interval τ is an individual that displays purposive behavior in time-interval τ.

DEC 12   "x is a psychological individual in time-interval τ" = df.

"for some y and for some **K**, **F**, **G**, and **H**, x is a
K(FG)-for-**H**[y] psychological individual in time-
interval τ"

Thus, it is possible for an individual to be a psychological individual at
some particular time but not at others. If an individual displays purposive
behavior at a given time, it is then a psychological individual; but at another
time that same individual may not be displaying purposive behavior, and
would at that time not be a psychological individual of one type (e.g., K(FG)-
for-H[y]) at one time and a psychological individual of another type (e.g.,
L(MN)-for-J[b]) at another. Indeed, we can imagine someone being a psychological individual of several types, even of many types, simultaneously. We
can now understand a situation that is analogous to that described by the
expression "he is irrational when it comes to that matter." This would be the
case of a person who is, with respect to the matter in question, not a psychological individual. Thus, the test of psychological individualness is the ability
to display purposive behavior or its index. Indeed, it is conceivable that such
diverse entities as a human being, another primate, a dog, a bear, an ant, a
bee, or a computer operating under the control of the proper sort of program
might be construed to be displaying purposive behavior according to this
definition, and thus to be a psychological individual.

DEC 13   "x exhibits **K(FG)**-for-**H**[b] decision behavior in time-
          interval τ" = df.

          "x exhibits purposive **K(FG)**-for-**H**[b] behavior in time-
          interval τ"

DEC 14   "x exhibits decision behavior in time-interval τ" = df.

          "x exhibits purposive behavior in time-interval τ"

Decision behavior is simply another name for *purposive behavior.* It can
therefore be inferred that if decision behavior has been displayed, then a
decision has been made and is being acted upon. *Pseudo decision behavior*
is exhibited by an individual when that individual behaves and nonveridically
(i.e., erroneously) believes that that behavior is decision behavior. *Pseudo*
K(FG)-for-H[b] *decision behavior* has been displayed by that individual when
it nonveridically believes that it has been displaying K(FG)-for-H[b] decision
behavior. Thus, an individual may erroneously believe that it has made a
decision of one sort (e.g., K(FG)-for-H[b]) or about one thing, while it may

not have made a decision at all, or, possibly unaware, it may even have made a decision about an entirely different matter.

DEC 15 "x exhibits pseudo **K**(**FG**)-for-**H**[b] decision behavior in time-interval τ" = df.

"x exhibits behavior in time-interval τ *and* x has nonveridical belief, in time-interval τ, that x exhibits **K**(**FG**)-for-**H**[b] decision behavior in time-interval τ"

DEC 16 "x exhibits pseudo decision behavior in time-interval τ" = df.

"x exhibits behavior in time-interval τ *and* x has nonveridical belief, in time-interval τ, that x exhibits decision behavior in time-interval τ"

Conscious decision behavior has been displayed by individual *x* if *x* veridically believes that it is displaying decision behavior. In general, *to be conscious* of something is to veridically believe it.

DEC 17 "x exhibits conscious **K**(**FG**)-for-**H**[b] decision behavior in time-interval τ" = df.

"x has veridical belief, in time-interval τ, that x exhibits **K**(**FG**)-for-**H**[b] decision behavior in time-interval τ"

DEC 18 "x exhibits conscious decision behavior in time-interval τ" = df.

"x has veridical belief, in time-interval τ, that x exhibits decision behavior in time-interval τ"

Unconscious decision behavior is exhibited by *x* if *x* exhibits decision behavior and does not believe at that time that it is decision behavior. So, *to be unconscious* of something is to be unaware of it, or not to believe that it is occurring.

DEC 19 "x exhibits unconscious decision behavior in time-interval τ" = df.

"x exhibits decision behavior in time-interval τ *and* x does not believe, in time-interval τ, that x exhibits decision behavior in time-interval τ"

We turn now to the definitions of events that affect the attainment of a goal by a psychological individual. The event can be conducive to attainment or nonattainment of a particular goal of a psychological individual, or the event can have neither effect.

DEC 20   "x is an event that is **K(FG)**-for-**H**[b] cooperative for y in time-interval τ" = df.

"y is a **K(FG)**-for-**H**[b] psychological individual in time-interval τ *and* there are time-intervals τ' and τ'' such that τ' is an earlier-and-discrete time-interval relative to τ'' *and* x is an event *and* x is part of time-interval τ' *and* x conduces to: the z that is the interval-part of b in τ'' has **H**"

DEC 20 says that there is an individual *b*, which may or may not be a person, that exists at least during the time-interval τ''. Moreover, individual *y* is a K(FG)-for-H[b] psychological individual in time-interval τ, which encompasses time-interval τ''. That is, a goal of individual *y* is that *b* have H in time-interval τ. Event *x* occurs in time-interval τ', which is also encompassed by time-interval τ'' but which is earlier than and nonverlapping with time-interval τ''. The occurrence of *x* in time-interval τ' conduces to (increases the likelihood of) z (which is that part of *b* that exists in time-interval τ'') having H, that is, to *b* having H in time-interval τ''. Since *x* is an event, there is no implication of intent on the part of *x*. The simple fact that *x*'s occurrence has a certain consequence for z suffices for the satisfaction of this definition. Event *x* is K(FG)-for-H[b] cooperative for *y* because *y* is a K(FG)-for-H[b] psychological individual and *x* is conducive to *b* having H and K in the proper time-intervals.

DEC 21 generalizes DEC 20. If event *x* conduces to the attainment of any goal of *y* in time-interval τ, then *x* is an event that is cooperative for *y* in that time-interval.

DEC 21   "x is an event that is cooperative for y in time-interval τ" = df.

"for some z and for some **K, F, G,** and **H**, x is an event that is **K(FG)**-for-**H**[z] cooperative for y in time-interval τ"

DEC 22 and DEC 23, which parallel DEC 20 and DEC 21, define a K(FG)-for-H[b] conflicting event and its generalization, respectively. The only difference between DEC 20 and DEC 22 is that whereas the definiens of DEC 20 contains the phrase "*x* conduces to: the *z* that is the interval-part of *b* in τ″ has ʜ," the definiens of DEC 22 contains the phrase "*x* conduces to: the *z* that is the interval-part of *b* in τ″ does not have ʜ." DEC 23 incorporates DEC 22 instead of DEC 20, which is incorporated into DEC 21.

DEC 22   "x is an event that is **K(FG)**-for-**H**[b] conflicting with y in time-interval τ" = df.

"y is a **K(FG)**-for-**H**[b] psychological individual in time-interval τ *and* there are time-intervals τ′ and τ″ such that each is part of τ *and* τ′ is earlier than and discrete from τ″ *and* x is an event *and* x conduces to: the z that is the interval-part of b in τ″ does not have **H**"

DEC 23   "x is an event that conflicts with y in time-interval τ" = df.

"for some z and for some **K, F, G,** and **H,** x is an event that is **K(FG)**-for-**H**[z] conflicting with y in time-interval τ"

DEC 24 and DEC 25 are concerned with *teleological independence*. This is the situation when, either with respect to a particular goal of psychological individual *y* or with respect to any goal of *y*, event *x* is neither cooperative nor conflicting.

DEC 24   "x is an event that is **K(FG)**-for-**H**[b] teleologically independent for y in time-interval τ" = df.

"x is an event that is not **K(FG)**-for-**H**[b] cooperative for y in time-interval τ *and* x is an event that is not **K(FG)**-for-**H**[b] conflicting for y in time-interval τ"

DEC 25   "x is an event that is teleologically independent for y in time-interval τ" = df.

"x is an event that is not cooperative for y in time-interval τ *and* x is an event that is not conflicting for y in time-interval τ"

The primary difference between a cooperative event (DEC 20) and a conflicting event (DEC 22) has to do with the effect of the occurrence of the event on the likelihood of attainment of person y's goal, H[b]. The occurrence of a cooperative event x conduces to the attainment of H[b], in contrast to what would have taken place in the absence of the occurrence of x, while the occurrence of a conflicting event conduces to the nonattainment of H[b]. A teleologically independent event has no effect on the attainment of H[b].

A *group* consists of at least two individuals that are psychological individuals in the same time-interval.

DEC 26   "x is a group in time-interval τ" = df.

"(there is a w and there is a w' such that both w and w' are psychological individuals in time-interval τ *and* w is part of x *and* w' is part of x) *and* (for all y, y is a psychological individual in time-interval τ *and* (for all w and for all w', (*if* w is part of y *and* w' is part of y *and* both w and w' are psychological individuals in time-interval τ, *then* w overlaps w')) *and* (there is a z such that *if* z is part of y *and* z is part of x, *then* y is part of x)) *and* (for all z, *if* z overlaps x, *then* (there is a u such that u is a psychological individual in time-interval τ *and* z overlaps u))"

DEC 27–29 introduce the notion of *making a statement:*

1. For person x to make statement p to person y is for x to perform an action m, whose goal is that y believes that p, *and*
2. x's action is not a case in point but is symbolic of a significant relation that stands between m and y's belief that p.

DEC 27   "person x makes statement 'p' to person y in time-interval τ" = df.

"person x exhibits purposive **K(FG)**-for-(y believes, in time-interval τ, that p) behavior in time-interval τ"

DEC 28   "person x agrees on 'p' with person y in time-interval τ" = df.

"person y makes statement 'p' to person x in time-interval τ *and* person x believes in time-interval τ that p"

For *x* to agree with *y* is for *x* to believe what *y* states.

DEC 29   "persons x and y mutually agree on 'p' in time-interval
          τ" = df.

          "person x agrees on 'p' with person y in time-interval τ *and*
          person y agrees on 'p' with person x in time-interval τ"

Thus, we have constructed and illustrated definitions relating to purpose, decision, and psychological individual (which can be read as "person") and to events that are cooperative, conflicting, and teleologically independent for psychological individuals. Finally, we have constructed the definition of *group*. In the next chapter these definitions will be used as building blocks of definitions relating to social interactions among psychological individuals.

5

Socioeconomic Definitions

Cooperation, Conflict, and Teleological Independence

The socioeconomic definitions are built around three central concepts: cooperation, conflict, and teleological independence. These concepts deal with the effect of the occurrence of an event, or of the behavior of a person, on the attainment of a goal by another person. The event or behavior is spoken of as being cooperative, conflicting, or teleologically independent for the person whose goal attainment is the matter of concern. Moreover, except in the most general forms of cooperation, conflict, and teleological independence, the goal and the means to its attainment are specified.

Thus, with respect to some goal of another person, an event or some behavior is cooperative for (or with) that other person if the occurrence of that event or behavior is conducive to (increases the probability of) the attainment of that goal of the other person; an event or some behavior is conflicting for (or with) that other person if the occurrence of that event or behavior is conducive to the nonattainment of that goal by the other person; and an event or some behavior is teleologically independent if its occurrence is neither cooperative nor conflicting with respect to the attainment of that goal. In this set of definitions, as with most of the others, intent is not directly dealt with, though it may be inferred. We may speak of *deliberate* or *nondeliberate* cooperation, conflict, or teleological independence. Cooperation, conflict, and teleological independence are seen not as manifestations of mental states but as events or behaviors that have certain sorts of consequences.

Our earlier formulation of these three types of events (DEC 20–25) and of purposive behavior (DEC 8) enables us to build up to such families of social concepts as cooperation, conflict, and teleologically neutral behavior. Thus, *cooperation* occurs when an individual acts so that his or her purposive behavior facilitates the attainment of the goal of the purposive behavior of another individual. Note that this general concept implies nothing about the mutuality of cooperation or about the relevant beliefs held by the cooperator. That is, the cooperation of individual *a* with individual *b* does not imply the cooperation of *b* with *a*. Nor does the fact of *a*'s cooperation with *b* imply *a*'s awareness of so doing. If each is cooperating with the other, we have *mutual cooperation*. If *a* is cooperating and is unaware of it (i.e., does not hold the belief that he is cooperating), then *a* is *unconsciously cooperating*. If it is *a*'s purpose not merely to behave in the fashion that turns out to be cooperative with *b*, but also to be thus cooperative, then *a* is *intentionally cooperating*. *Symmetric mutual cooperation* occurs when the behavior and desired states of two mutually cooperating persons are not the same. As we shall see, other, more detailed variations of cooperation can be developed.

For example, if Fred is mopping the kitchen floor and his wife, Alice, is deliberately staying out of the kitchen, she is cooperating with him. Moreover, if Alice is aware that Fred is mopping the floor and if she is avoiding the kitchen for that very reason, she is intentionally cooperating with him. But if her reason for staying out of the kitchen is to avoid the temptations of cookie jar and refrigerator in pursuit of a trimmer waistline, and if she is not even aware of what Fred is up to, then her cooperation is unconscious. In either event, the fact that Fred's activity furthers Alice's dietary ambitions causes him also to be cooperating with her (as would not be the case if she had no such ambitions); their cooperation is therefore both mutual and symmetric.

Our earlier definition of *event* provides a foundation for what follows. Clearly, for an *event* to be cooperative, conflicting, or teleologically independent, it must be viewed in relation to a psychological individual and the psychological individual's goals. In order to speak of the cooperation, conflict, or teleological independence of a psychological individual, we construe the behavior of a psychological individual that is cooperative, in conflict, or teleologically independent for another, as the event. Thus, we have two psychological individuals, and this means that we have the goal states of each to consider. The two psychological individuals could be completely disparate both in terms of goals and means (i.e., x is K(FG)-for-H[a] and y is L(MN)-for-J[b]), in which case we speak of cooperation, conflict, or teleological independence. They could instead share a goal but be disparate as to means (x is K(FG)-for-H[a] and y is L(MN)-for-H[a]), in which case we can speak of *convergent* cooperation, conflict, or teleological independence. If they employ the same means in pursuit of disparate goals (x is K(FG)-for-H[a] and y is K(FG)-for-J[b]), we can speak of *divergent* cooperation, conflict, or teleological independence. They may share an identical goal and its associated means (x is K(FG)-for-H[a] and so is y), in which case we speak of cooperation or teleological independence *in concert,* or of *unintended* conflict. Finally, if they employ the same means *and* the goal of one psychological individual is the negation of the goal of the other (i.e., x is K(FG)-for-H[a] and y is K(FG)-for-not-H[a]) *and* there is conflict (x's behavior conduces to the nonoccurrence of H[a], or to the occurrence of not-H[a]), then we speak of *head-on* conflict.[1]

The Definitions

Simple Cooperation (SOC 1–6)

SOC 1   "x is a person who cooperates **L(MN)**-for-**J**[b] with person y **K(FG)**-for-**H**[a] in time-interval τ" = df.

"x exhibits overt purposive **L(MN)**-for-**J**[b] behavior in time-interval τ *and* there is a z that is the interval-part of x in time-interval τ *and* z is an event that is **K(FG)**-for-**H**[a] cooperative with y in time-interval τ"

SOC 2   "x is a person who cooperates **L(MN)**-for-**H**[a] convergently with person y **K(FG)**-for-**H**[a] in time-interval τ" = df.

"x is a person who cooperates **L(MN)**-for-**H**[a] with person y **K(FG)**-for-**H**[a] in time-interval τ"

1. It would be well to describe here, in some detail, a set of terms that will hereafter be employed in reference to certain aspects of these socioeconomic definitions:

Type refers to the polarity of the social behavior described in the definition. (Is the behavior cooperative, conflicting, or teleologically independent?)

Means and *ends* refer to the means and ends of the behavior. (Means are the "K(FG)" in " K(FG)-for-H[a]," while the ends are "H[a].")

Style refers to the degree of match between the means and ends of the person displaying behavior of a given type and those of the person who is the object of the behavior. (Style can take on such values as convergent, divergent, in concert, unintended, or head-on.)

Mode refers to variations in the match between the types, styles, means, and/or ends of the behaviors of the two persons engaged in mutual behavior. (Mode can take on the values symmetric, quasi-symmetric, or asymmetric.)

SOC 3   "x is a person who cooperates $\mathbf{K}(\mathbf{FG})$-for-$\mathbf{J}$[b]
divergently with person y $\mathbf{K}(\mathbf{FG})$-for-$\mathbf{H}$[a] in time-
interval τ" = df.

"x is a person who cooperates $\mathbf{K}(\mathbf{FG})$-for-$\mathbf{J}$[b] with person
y $\mathbf{K}(\mathbf{FG})$-for-$\mathbf{H}$[a] in time-interval τ"

SOC 4   "x is a person who cooperates $\mathbf{K}(\mathbf{FG})$-for-$\mathbf{H}$[a] in concert
with person y in time-interval τ" = df.

"x is a person who cooperates $\mathbf{K}(\mathbf{FG})$-for-$\mathbf{H}$[a] with person y $\mathbf{K}(\mathbf{FG})$-for-$\mathbf{H}$[a] in time-interval τ"

SOC 5   "x is a person who accommodatingly cooperates with
person y $\mathbf{K}(\mathbf{FG})$-for-$\mathbf{H}$[a] in time-interval τ" = df.

"for some predicates $\mathbf{L}$, $\mathbf{M}$, $\mathbf{N}$, and $\mathbf{J}$ *and* some person z,
x is a person who cooperates $\mathbf{L}(\mathbf{MN})$-for-$\mathbf{J}$[z] with person
y $\mathbf{K}(\mathbf{FG})$-for-$\mathbf{H}$[a] in time-interval τ"

SOC 6   "x is a person who cooperates with person y in time-interval
τ" = df.

"for some predicates $\mathbf{K}$, $\mathbf{F}$, $\mathbf{G}$, and $\mathbf{H}$ *and* some person w,
x is a person who accommodatingly cooperates with person
y $\mathbf{K}(\mathbf{FG})$-for-$\mathbf{H}$[w] in time-interval τ"

Simple Conflict (SOC 7–13)

When we turn to the case of a conflicting person, we find four situations that
are analogous to those for a cooperating person, plus one other. Again, the
differences depend on the nature of the match between means and goals
of the two persons. If x is K(FG)-for-H[a] while y is K(FG)-for-H[a], we have
conflict *in parallel*. If x is L(MN)-for-H[a] and y is K(FG)-for-H[a], we
have *convergent* conflict. If x is K(FG)-for-J[b] and y is K(FG)-for-H[a],
we have *divergent* conflict. But if x is K(FG)-for-not-H[a] and y is K(FG)-for-
H[a], we have a strange case. How can there be conflict when two persons
are using the same means in pursuit of the same ends? Is there conflict when
two fielders, both chasing the same fly ball, collide? Indeed there is. If one
fielder chases the ball unaware that the other fielder is also chasing it, and the
second fielder prevents the first from catching the fly, we are safe in speaking
of conflict. We call this *unintended* conflict. Thus:

SOC 7 "x is a person who conflicts **L**(**MN**)-for-**J**[b] with person y **K**(**FG**)-for-**H**[a] in time-interval τ" = df.

"x exhibits overt purposive **L**(**MN**)-for-**J**[b] behavior in time-interval τ *and* there is a z that is the interval-part of x in time-interval τ *and* z is an event that is **K**(**FG**)-for-**H**[a] conflicting with y in time-interval τ"

SOC 8 "x is a person who conflicts **L**(**MN**)-for-**H**[a] convergently with person y **K**(**FG**)-for-**H**[a] in time-interval τ" = df.

"x is a person who conflicts **L**(**MN**)-for-**H**[a] with person y **K**(**FG**)-for-**H**[a] in time-interval τ"

SOC 9 "x is a person who conflicts **K**(**FG**)-for-**J**[b] divergently with person y **K**(**FG**)-for-**H**[a] in time-interval τ" = df.

"x is a person who conflicts **K**(**FG**)-for-**J**[b] with person y **K**(**FG**)-for-**H**[a] in time-interval τ"

SOC 10 "x is a person who conflicts **K**(**FG**)-for-**H**[a] in parallel with person y in time-interval τ" = df.

"x is a person who conflicts **K**(**FG**)-for-**H**[a] with person y **K**(**FG**)-for-**H**[a] in time-interval τ"

SOC 11 "x is a person who is in head-on conflict with person y **K**(**FG**)-for-**H**[a] in time-interval τ" = df.

"x is a person who conflicts **K**(**FG**)-for-not-**H**[a] with person y **K**(**FG**)-for-**H**[a] in time-interval τ"

SOC 12 "x is a person who conflicts with person y **K**(**FG**)-for-**H**[a] in time-interval τ" = df.

"for some predicates **L**, **M**, **N**, and **J** *and* some person z, x is a person who conflicts **L**(**MN**)-for-**J**[z] with person y **K**(**FG**)-for-**H**[a] in time-interval τ"

SOC 13 "x is a person who conflicts with person y in time-interval τ" = df.

"for some predicates **K**, **F**, **G**, and **H** *and* some person
w, x is a person who conflicts with person y **K**(**FG**)-for-
H[w] in time-interval τ"

Simple Teleological Independence (SOC 14–19)

Teleological independence follows the same pattern as does cooperation.
Thus:

SOC 14   "x is a person who is teleologically independent **L**(**MN**)-
for-**J**[b] for person y **K**(**FG**)-for-**H**[a] in time-interval
τ" = df.

"x exhibits overt purposive **L**(**MN**)-for-**J**[b] behavior in
time-interval τ *and* there is a z that is the interval-part of x
in time-interval τ *and* z is an event that is **K**(**FG**)-for-
H[a] teleologically independent for y in time-interval τ"

SOC 15   "x is a person who is teleologically independent **L**(**MN**)-
for-**H**[a] convergently for person y **K**(**FG**)-for-**H**[a] in
time-interval τ" = df.

"x is a person who is teleologically independent **L**(**MN**)-
for-**H**[a] for person y **K**(**FG**)-for-**H**[a] in time-
interval τ"

SOC 16   "x is a person who is teleologically independent **K**(**FG**)-
for-**J**[b] divergently for person y **K**(**FG**)-for-**H**[a] in
time-interval τ" = df.

"x is a person who is teleologically independent **K**(**FG**)-
for-**J**[b] for person y **K**(**FG**)-for-**H**[a] in time-interval τ"

SOC 17   "x is a person who is teleologically independent **K**(**FG**)-
for-**H**[a] in concert with person y in time-interval τ" = df.

"x is a person who is teleologically independent **K**(**FG**)-
for-**H**[a] for person y **K**(**FG**)-for-**H**[a] in time-
interval τ"

SOC 18   "x is a person who is teleologically independent with
person y **K**(**FG**)-for-**H**[a] in time-interval τ" = df.

"for some predicates **L**, **M**, **N**, and **J**, person x is teleologically independent **L(MN)**-for-**J**[b] for person y in time-interval τ"

SOC 19   "x is a person who is teleologically independent with person y in time-interval τ" = df.

"for some predicates **K**, **F**, **G**, and **H** *and* some person w, x is a person who is teleologically independent with person y **K(FG)**-for-**H**[a] in time-interval τ"

Deliberateness (SOC 20–33)

In constructing our socioeconomic definitions, *deliberateness* becomes an operator that may be attached to cooperating, conflicting, or teleologically independent persons who veridically believe (i.e., know) that they are such. Thus:

SOC 20   "x is a person who deliberately cooperates **L(MN)**-for-**J**[b] with person y **K(FG)**-for-**H**[a] in time-interval τ" = df.

"x is a person who cooperates **L(MN)**-for-**J**[b] with person y **K(FG)**-for-**H**[a] in time-interval τ *and* x veridically believes that x is a person who cooperates **L(MN)**-for-**J**[b] with person y **K(FG)**-for-**H**[a] in time-interval τ"

Deliberateness requires that the deliberator veridically believe that he is acting as he is at the time he acts. Were he to believe this at a time other than when the act takes place, then the act would not be deliberate. If *x*'s belief that he is a person who cooperates L(MN)-for-J[b], etc., is an erroneous (nonveridical) belief, then we can say that *x* is under the illusion that he cooperates L(MN)-for-J[b], etc. So to be deliberate in an action is to know at the time of the act that one is so acting. Later we will look into the effect of time differences on deliberateness and on other aspects of cooperation, conflict, and teleological independence. The "deliberateness" operator can be applied to SOC 1–19 as follows:

SOC 21   "x is a person who deliberately cooperates **L(MN)**-for-**H**[a] convergently with person y **K(FG)**-for-**H**[a] in time-interval τ" = df.

"x is a person who deliberately cooperates **L**(**MN**)-for-**H**[a] with person y **K**(**FG**)-for-**H**[a] in time-interval τ"

SOC 22 "x is a person who deliberately cooperates **K**(**FG**)-for-**J**[b] divergently with person y **K**(**FG**)-for-**H**[a] in time-interval τ" = df.

"x is a person who deliberately cooperates **K**(**FG**)-for-**J**[b] with person y **K**(**FG**)-for-**H**[a] in time-interval τ"

SOC 23 "x is a person who deliberately cooperates **K**(**FG**)-for-**H**[a] in concert with person y in time-interval τ" = df.

"x is a person who deliberately cooperates **K**(**FG**)-for-**H**[a] with person y **K**(**FG**)-for-**H**[a] in time-interval τ"

SOC 24 "x is a person who deliberately cooperates with person y in time-interval τ" = df.

"for some predicates **K**, **F**, **G**, **H**, **L**, **M**, **N**, and **J** *and* for some persons w and z, x is a person who deliberately cooperates **L**(**MN**)-for-**J**[b] with person y **K**(**FG**)-for-**H**[a] in time-interval τ"

SOC 25 "x is a person who deliberately conflicts **L**(**MN**)-for-**J**[b] with person y **K**(**FG**)-for-**H**[a] in time-interval τ" = df.

"x is a person who conflicts **L**(**MN**)-for-**J**[b] with person y **K**(**FG**)-for-**H**[a] in time-interval τ *and* x veridically believes that x is a person who conflicts **L**(**MN**)-for-**J**[b] with person y **K**(**FG**)-for-**H**[a] in time-interval τ"

SOC 26 "x is a person who deliberately conflicts **L**(**MN**)-for-**H**[a] convergently with person y **K**(**FG**)-for-**H**[a] in time-interval τ" = df.

"x is a person who deliberately conflicts **L**(**MN**)-for-**H**[a] with person y **K**(**FG**)-for-**H**[a] in time-interval τ"

SOC 27 "x is a person who deliberately conflicts **K**(**FG**)-for-**J**[b] divergently with person y **K**(**FG**)-for-**H**[a] in time-interval τ" = df.

"x is a person who deliberately conflicts **K**(**FG**)-for-**J**[b] with person y **K**(**FG**)-for-**H**[a] in time-interval τ"

SOC 28   "x is a person who is deliberately in head-on conflict **K**(**FG**)-for-not-**H**[a] with person y **K**(**FG**)-for-**H**[a] in time-interval τ" = df.

"x is a person who deliberately conflicts **K**(**FG**)-for-not-**H**[a] with person y **K**(**FG**)-for-**H**[a] in time-interval τ"

SOC 29   "x is a person who deliberately conflicts with person y in time-interval τ" = df.

"for some predicates **K**, **F**, **G**, **H**, **L**, **M**, **N**, and **J** *and* for some persons w and z, x is a person who deliberately conflicts **L**(**MN**)-for-**J**[b] with person y **K**(**FG**)-for-**H**[a] in time-interval τ"

SOC 30   "x is a person who is deliberately teleologically independent **L**(**MN**)-for-**J**[b] for person y **K**(**FG**)-for-**H**[a] in time-interval τ" = df.

"x is a person who is teleologically independent **L**(**MN**)-for-**J**[b] for person y **K**(**FG**)-for-**H**[a] in time-interval τ *and* x veridically believes that x is a person who is teleologically independent **L**(**MN**)-for-**J**[b] for person y **K**(**FG**)-for-**H**[a] in time-interval τ"

SOC 31   "x is a person who is deliberately teleologically independent **L**(**MN**)-for-**H**[a] convergently for person y **K**(**FG**)-for-**H**[a] in time-interval τ" = df.

"x is a person who is deliberately teleologically independent **L**(**MN**)-for-**H**[a] for person y **K**(**FG**)-for-**H**[a] in time-interval τ"

SOC 32   "x is a person who is deliberately teleologically independent **K**(**FG**)-for-**J**[b] divergently for person y **K**(**FG**)-for-**H**[a] in time-interval τ" = df.

"x is a person who is deliberately teleologically independent **K**(**FG**)-for-**J**[b] for person y **K**(**FG**)-for-**H**[a] in time-interval τ"

SOC 33   "x is a person who is deliberately teleologically
          independent $\mathbf{K(FG)}$-for-$\mathbf{H}$[a] in concert for person y in
          time-interval τ" = df.

          "x is a person who is deliberately teleologically independent
          $\mathbf{K(FG)}$-for-$\mathbf{H}$[a] with person y $\mathbf{K(FG)}$-for-$\mathbf{H}$[a] in
          time-interval τ"

Symmetric Mutuality (SOC 34–46)

If both *x* and *y* are cooperating, we have *mutual* cooperation. Again, the same
changes and combinations found in SOC 1–19 can be carried out for the case
of mutual cooperation.

Definitions SOC 1–33 are concerned with the behavior of one person as it
affects the ability of another to attain his or her ends. We can now consider
cases of two persons, each behaving in ways that might affect the ability of
the other to attain his or her goals. All such cases bear the qualifying label
mutual. Mutual teleologically involved behavior can be of three general
modes: symmetric, quasi-symmetric, or asymmetric. Symmetric behaviors
are those in which both persons display the same type of behavior (cooperation, conflict, or teleological independence) of the same *style* (convergent,
divergent, in concert, unintended, or head-on) with respect to the same set of
means and *ends* (e.g., K(FG)-for-H[a]). SOC 34–46 are examples of symmetric mutual behavior.

SOC 34   "x and y symmetrically mutually cooperate $\mathbf{L(MN)}$-for-
          $\mathbf{J}$[b], $\mathbf{K(FG)}$-for-$\mathbf{H}$[a], in time-interval τ" = df.

          "x is a person who cooperates $\mathbf{L(MN)}$-for-$\mathbf{J}$[b] with per-
          son y $\mathbf{K(FG)}$-for-$\mathbf{H}$[a] in time-interval τ *and* y is a person
          who   cooperates $\mathbf{K(FG)}$-for-$\mathbf{H}$[a]   with   person   x
          $\mathbf{L(MN)}$-for-$\mathbf{J}$[b] in time-interval τ"

SOC 35   "x and y symmetrically mutually cooperate $\mathbf{L(MN)}$-for-
          $\mathbf{H}$[a], $\mathbf{K(FG)}$-for-$\mathbf{H}$[a], convergently in time-interval τ"
          = df.

          "x and y symmetrically mutually cooperate $\mathbf{L(MN)}$-for-
          $\mathbf{H}$[a], $\mathbf{K(FG)}$-for-$\mathbf{H}$[a], in time-interval τ"

SOC 36   "x and y symmetrically mutually cooperate $\mathbf{K(FG)}$-for-
          $\mathbf{J}$[b], $\mathbf{K(FG)}$-for-$\mathbf{H}$[a], divergently in time-interval τ"
          = df.

"x and y symmetrically mutually cooperate **K**(**FG**)-for-**J**[b], **K**(**FG**)-for-**H**[a], in time-interval τ"

SOC 37 "x and y symmetrically mutually cooperate **K**(**FG**)-for-**H**[a] in concert in time-interval τ" = df.

"x and y symmetrically mutually cooperate **K**(**FG**)-for-**H**[a], **K**(**FG**)-for-**H**[a], in time-interval τ"

SOC 38 "x and y symmetrically mutually conflict **L**(**MN**)-for-**J**[b], **K**(**FG**)-for-**H**[a], in time-interval τ" = df.

"x is a person who conflicts **L**(**MN**)-for-**J**[b] with person y **K**(**FG**)-for-**H**[a] in time-interval τ *and* y is a person who conflicts **K**(**FG**)-for-**H**[a] with person x **L**(**MN**)-for-**J**[b] in time-interval τ"

SOC 39 "x and y symmetrically mutually conflict **L**(**MN**)-for-**H**[a], **K**(**FG**)-for-**H**[a], convergently in time-interval τ" = df.

"x and y symmetrically mutually conflict **L**(**MN**)-for-**H**[a], **K**(**FG**)-for-**H**[a], in time-interval τ"

SOC 40 "x and y symmetrically mutually conflict **K**(**FG**)-for-**J**[b], **K**(**FG**)-for-**H**[a], divergently in time-interval τ" = df.

"x and y symmetrically mutually conflict **K**(**FG**)-for-**J**[b], **K**(**FG**)-for-**H**[a], in time-interval τ"

SOC 41 "x and y are in symmetric mutual competition **K**(**FG**)-for-**H**[a] in time-interval τ" = df.

"x and y symmetrically mutually conflict **K**(**FG**)-for-**H**[a], **K**(**FG**)-for-**H**[a], in time-interval τ"

SOC 42 "x and y symmetrically mutually conflict **K**(**FG**)-for-**H**[a], **K**(**FG**)-for-not-**H**[a], head-on in time-interval τ" = df.

"x and y symmetrically mutually conflict **K**(**FG**)-for-**H**[a], **K**(**FG**)-for-not-**H**[a], in time-interval τ"

SOC 43   "x and y are symmetrically mutually teleologically
         independent **L**(**MN**)-for-**J**[b], **K**(**FG**)-for-**H**[a], in
         time-interval τ" = df.

         "x is a person who is teleologically independent **L**(**MN**)-
         for-**J**[b] with person y **K**(**FG**)-for-**H**[a] in time-interval
         τ *and* y is a person who is teleologically independent
         K(**FG**)-for-**H**[a] with person x **L**(**MN**)-for-**J**[b] in
         time-interval τ"

SOC 44   "x and y are symmetrically mutually teleologically
         independent **L**(**MN**)-for-**H**[a], **K**(**FG**)-for-**H**[a],
         convergently in time-interval τ" = df.

         "x and y are symmetrically mutually teleologically indepen-
         dent **L**(**MN**)-for-**H**[a], **K**(**FG**)-for-**H**[a], in time-
         interval τ"

SOC 45   "x and y are symmetrically mutually teleologically
         independent **K**(**FG**)-for-**J**[b], **K**(**FG**)-for-**H**[a],
         divergently in time-interval τ" = df.

         "x and y are symmetrically mutually teleologically indepen-
         dent **K**(**FG**)-for-**J**[b], **K**(**FG**)-for-**H**[a], in time-
         interval τ"

SOC 46   "x and y are symmetrically mutually teleologically
         independent **K**(**FG**)-for-**H**[a], **K**(**FG**)-for-**H**[a], in
         concert in time-interval τ" = df.

         "x and y are symmetrically mutually teleologically indepen-
         dent **K**(**FG**)-for-**H**[a], **K**(**FG**)-for-**H**[a], in time-
         interval τ"

Quasi-Symmetric Mutuality (SOC 47–49)

Quasi-symmetric mutual behavior is mutual behavior in which both persons
display the same type of behavior of the same style, but their behaviors differ
with respect to means, ends, or both. Two examples are given here:

SOC 47   "x **L**(**MN**)-for-**J**[b] *and* **K**(**FG**)-for-**H**[a], *and* y
         O(**PQ**)-for-**I**[c] *and* **R**(**ST**)-for-**U**[d], are persons who

are quasi-symmetrically mutually cooperating in time-interval τ" = df.

"x is a person who cooperates **L(MN)**-for-**H**[a] with person y **K(FG)**-for-**H**[a] in time-interval τ *and* y is a person who cooperates **O(PQ)**-for-**I**[c] with person x **R(ST)**-for-**U**[d] in time-interval τ"

SOC 48   "x **L(MN)**-for-**J**[b] *and* **L(MN)**-for-**H**[a], *and* y
          O(PQ)-for-**I**[c] *and* **O(PQ)**-for-**F**[d], are persons who
          are quasi-symmetrically mutually conflicting divergently in
          time-interval τ" = df.

          "x is a person who conflicts **L(MN)**-for-**J**[b] divergently
          with person y **L(MN)**-for-**H**[a] in time-interval τ *and* y
          is a person who conflicts **O(PQ)**-for-**I**[c] divergently with
          person x **O(PQ)**-for-**F**[d] in time-interval τ"

Quasi-symmetric mutual behavior also extends to teleological independence and can appear in the variations that occur in SOC 34–46. *Asymmetric mutual behavior* is mutual behavior in which the types of behavior (cooperative, conflicting, or teleologically independent behavior), or the styles, or both, as well as means and/or ends, differ. For example:

SOC 49   "x and y are asymmetrically mutually interacting persons,
          x cooperating **L(MN)**-for-**J**[b] with y **K(FG)**-for-**J**[b]
          convergently, y conflicting **R(ST)**-for-not-**F**[d] with x
          R(ST)-for-**F**[d] head-on in time-interval τ" = df.

          "x is a person who cooperates **L(MN)**-for-**J**[b] convergently with person y **K(FG)**-for-**J**[b] in time-interval τ
          and y is a person who is in head-on conflict **R(ST)**-for-not-**F**[d] with person x **R(ST)**-for-**F**[d] in time-interval τ"

Asymmetric mutual behavior can be found in combinations of cooperation, conflict, or teleological independence with uniform styles, or in combinations of different styles when both persons are cooperating, conflicting, or teleologically independent. The qualifier *deliberately mutually* signifies that there are two mutually interacting persons both of whom are behaving deliberately. That is, each of them veridically believes (i.e., knows) that he or she is behaving as he or she actually is. Each of the definitions SOC 34–

49 can be so modified to form many other definitions. In addition, by using the qualifier *semideliberate* we can deal with cases where one person is behaving deliberately and one is not.

Rivalry, Revenge, Avenging (SOC 50–52)

Rivalry is the state of affairs in which two persons are in symmetric mutual competition, or are disposed to be in some circumstances.

SOC 50   "x and y are $\mathbf{K(FG)}$-for-$\mathbf{H}$[a] rivals in time-interval τ"
= df.

"x and y are in symmetric mutual competition $\mathbf{K(FG)}$-for-$\mathbf{H}$[a] in time-interval τ *or* x and y satisfy an index of: x *and* y are in symmetric mutual competition $\mathbf{K(FG)}$-for-$\mathbf{H}$[a] in time-interval τ"

Definitions SOC 1–50 deal with social behavior that occurs in a time-interval τ. Definitions SOC 34–50 deal with mutual behavior—interval-simultaneous behavior of two persons that are cooperative, conflicting, or teleologically independent. Interval-simultaneity implies not literal occurrence at the same moment, but occurrence within the same time-interval. But since time-intervals do not have fixed length, with a sufficiently long interval all pairs of events could be interval-simultaneous pairs. However, since we are able to determine interval location and overlap, we can quite cleanly establish interval-nonsimultaneity. We will now consider definitions referring to two behaviors that occur in two distinct (nonoverlapping) time-intervals. That is, we consider interval-nonsimultaneous behaviors.

Person x takes revenge on, exacts vengeance from, or exacts restitution from person y if, at an earlier time, y has conflicted with x and then, at a given time, x deliberately conflicts with y.

SOC 51   "person x takes revenge on person y in time-interval τ'"
= df.

"τ is an earlier-and-discrete time-interval relative to τ' *and* y is a person who conflicts with person x in time-interval τ *and* x is a person who deliberately conflicts with person y in time-interval τ'"

SOC 52   "person x avenges person z on person y in time-interval τ"
= df.

"τ is an earlier-and-discrete time interval relative to τ' *and*
y is a person who conflicts with person z in time-interval τ
and x is a person who deliberately conflicts with person y
in time-interval τ'"

The difference between SOC 51 (taking revenge) and SOC 52 (avenging)
is that in the former case the injured party takes retaliatory action, while in
the latter case a third party, neither the offender nor the injured, engages in
retaliation.

An entire panoply of hostile interactions comes to mind at this point. Such
notions as *attack, ambush, gratuitous meddling, aggression,* and *hostility*
could easily be defined here. We refrain from doing so, but it is clear that
these definitions can be constructed.

Investment, Agreement, Contract, Payment, Trade (SOC 53–57)

We can now examine an entirely new set of definitions that appear similar to
mutual behaviors such as were defined in SOC 32–52, except that the two or
more behaviors (all cooperative, all conflicting, all teleologically independent, or mixed) do not all occur in the same time-interval. Five basic concepts
are presented in this section: *investment, agreement, contract, payment,* and
trade, some of which are presented in several variations or with several qual-
ifications.

For a person x to make a certain investment with person y is for x to
cooperate with y in time-interval τ and for x to expect that y will cooperate
with x in some time-interval τ', where τ is an earlier-and-discrete time-
interval with respect to τ'.

SOC 53   "person x makes a certain **K**(**FG**)-for-**H**[a] investment
          in time-interval τ with person y **L**(**MN**)-for-**J**[b] in time-
          interval τ'" = df.

          "x is a person who cooperates **K**(**FG**)-for-**H**[a] with per-
          son y **L**(**MN**)-for-**J**[b] in time-interval τ *and* person x
          expects, in time-interval τ, that y is a person who cooperates
          L(**MN**)-for-**J**[b] with person x **K**(**FG**)-for-**H**[a] in
          time-interval τ'"

For x and y to *mutually agree* is for each of them to agree with the other
on the same matter. An *agreement* is a mutual understanding as to mutually
advantageous actions to be taken by two persons. In a particular time-interval

τ, person *x* makes the statement to person *y* that *x* plans to behave, in a specific time-interval τ′, in a specific manner that is cooperative for *y,* and that *x* expects *y* to behave, in some time-interval τ″, in a specific manner that is cooperative for *x.* In the same time-interval τ, *y* states that he plans to behave, in time-interval τ″, in a specific manner that is cooperative for *x,* and that he expects that *x,* in time-interval τ′, will behave in a specific manner that is cooperative for *y.* It is clear that to have an agreement is much more complex than it is to mutually agree. An agreement implies that the two parties agree on *plans to act.*

SOC 54   "persons x and y enter into a **K(FG)**-for-**H**[a]-time-τ′, **L(MN)**-for-**J**[b]-time-τ″, agreement, in time-interval τ" = df.

"τ is an earlier-and-discrete time-interval relative to τ′ *and* τ is an earlier-and-discrete time-interval relative to τ″ *and* person x states, at time τ, that x plans to cooperate **L(MN)**-for-**J**[b] with person y, **K(FG)**-for-**H**[a] at time τ′ *and* person x states, at time τ, that x expects person y to cooperate **K(FG)**-for-**H**[a] with person x **L(MN)**-for-**J**[b] at time τ″ *and* person y states, at time τ, that y plans to cooperate **K(FG)**-for-**H**[a] with person x, **L(MN)**-for-**J**[b] at time τ″ *and* y expects person x to cooperate **L(MN)**-for-**J**[b] with person y **K(FG)**-for-**H**[a] at time τ′"

There are differences between those agreements that are fulfilled to the letter and those that are not. And there are differences between those agreements that are entered into with the intention of fulfillment and those that are not, as well as between those agreements entered into in the belief that the other party or parties will fulfill and those that are not.

An agreement is an extremely complex set of statements. When entering into an agreement, *x* and *y* each make two types of statements. One type is about one's own plans, and the other is about one's expectations of the other's plans. It is possible for each of these four statements to be made honestly or dishonestly. That is, *x* may state, honestly or dishonestly, that he plans to behave in a certain fashion (i.e., to deliver what has been agreed to or to pay the penalty). Moreover, *x* has expectations about *y*'s intentions. Similarly, *y* can make the same sorts of statements about his own plans and expectations. When all these expectations are taken into account, sixteen possible cases appear. Of these, there are six symmetrical pairs, so there are, in fact, ten distinct cases. All sixteen are shown in table 5.1. While it is not easy to generate simple titles for these agreement types (indeed, in some cases the titles are somewhat strained), the differences in agreement type are easily accommodated in the formal definitional schema.

In general, all sixteen agreement types can be generated by using "veridically" to correspond with the appearance of "honor" in the table and by using "nonveridically" to correspond with "break." Should the definitions for these agreement types be formally constructed, we would find that in each definition there are four places in which "veridically" or "nonveridically" appears. These correspond to the four columns in the table in which the words "honor" and "break" appear. (A further variation on the agreement, generating a concomitant additional number of agreement types, arises if we consider circumstances in which *x* or *y* or both do not know whether they themselves or the other party plans to honor the agreement.)

Completion of an agreement would be the state of affairs in which the agreement called for fulfillment in a time-interval earlier than and discrete from the given time, and when, in the given time, the behavior agreed to had been performed. For *x* to defraud *y* would be the state of affairs in which the agreement called for fulfillment in an earlier-and-discrete time period relative to the given time, and when, in the given time, *y* had fulfilled his commitment, but *x* had not and does not plan to.

A *payment* is an action that transfers from one person to another the means for the attainment of ends. As a result of a payment, the payer is in the same position as the object of conflicting action, while the recipient is in the same position as the object of cooperating action. So the payer can be said to have cooperated with the recipient, while the recipient has been in conflict with the payer.

SOC 55   "person x pays **K**(**FG**)-for-**H**[y] to person y in time-interval τ" = df.

"y is a person who conflicts **K**(**FG**)-for-**H**[y] with person x **K**(**FG**)-for-**H**[y] in time-interval τ *and* x is a person who cooperates **K**(**FG**)-for-**H**[y] with person y **K**(**FG**)-for-**H**[y] in time-interval τ"

Thus, the conflicting person (the recipient) conflicts in such a way as to lead to *y* (himself) having H, while the cooperating person (the payer) cooperates so as to lead to the same *y* having H. The payment is H. In this case, the predicate H is the ownership of the transferred rights or property.

Table 5.1   Agreement types, by intentions and expectations

Type	: Descriptive title	x : plans to	x expects y to	y plans to	y expects x to
1	: BOTH HONEST	: honor	honor	honor	honor
2	: HONEST y MISTRUSTS x	: honor	honor	honor	break
2a	: HONEST x MISTRUSTS y	: honor	break	honor	honor
3	: x VICTIM OF y	: honor	honor	break	honor
3a	: y VICTIM OF x	: break	honor	honor	honor
4	: y MISTRUSTS AND PROTECTS	: honor	honor	break	break
4a	: x MISTRUSTS AND PROTECTS	: break	break	honor	honor
5	: BILATERAL : HONEST : MISTRUST	: honor	break	honor	break
6	: KNOWING VICTIM x	: honor	break	break	honor
6a	: KNOWING VICTIM y	: break	honor	honor	break
7	: HONEST x KNOWS y PARANOID	: honor	break	break	break
7a	: HONEST y KNOWS x PARANOID	: break	break	honor	break
8	: SYMMETRIC : SELF-DECEIVING : CHEATS	: break	honor	break	honor
9	: BOTH CHEAT, ONLY y KNOWS x	: break	honor	break	break
9a	: BOTH CHEAT, ONLY x KNOWS y	: break	break	break	honor
10	: BOTH ARE THIEVES	: break	break	break	break

A *trade* is a pair of reciprocal payments. Ordinarily, if one of the payments is in the form of money, we refer to the trade as a *purchase*. But any transaction involving reciprocal exchange of assets is a trade.

SOC 56   "person x trades **H** in time-interval τ to person y for **J** in time-interval τ'" = df.

"person x pays **K(FG)**-for-**H**[y] to person y in time-interval τ *and* person y pays **L(MN)**-for-**J**[x] to person x in time-interval τ'"

SOC 57   "persons x and y enter into a **K(FG)**-for-**H**[a]-time-τ', **L(MN)**-for-**J**[b]-time-τ", contract, in time-interval τ, with penalties **R(ST)**-for-**U**[c], **O(PQ)**-for-**V**[d]" = df.

"persons x and y enter into a **K(FG)**-for-**H**[a]-time-τ', **L(MN)**-for-**J**[b]-time-τ", agreement, in time-interval τ *and* if, in time-interval τ', x does not cooperate **L(MN)**-for-**J**[b] with person y **K(FG)**-for-**H**[a] then person x pays **R(ST)**-for-**U**[y] to person y in time-interval τ', *and* if, in time-interval τ", y does not cooperate **K(FG)**-for-**H**[a] with person x **L(MN)**-for-**J**[b] then person y pays **O(PQ)**-for-**V**[x] to person x in time-interval τ'''"

A *contract* is a *mutual agreement* as to a certain investment. A contract is defined in terms of κ(FG)-for-H[a] and L(MN)-for-J[b] cooperative behavior, and penalty clauses: *x* to pay R to *y* in the event of *x*'s noncompliance with the contract, and *y* to pay s to *x* in the event of *y*'s noncompliance with the contract.

Moreover, plans or expectations (as defined in AUX 38–40) can take place with respect to cooperation, conflict, and teleological independence. Indeed, each person mentioned in SOC 1–57 can have the expectation that the behavior there defined will occur, and each actor mentioned in these fifty-seven definitions can have the plan or the expectation that the behavior will occur.

With these definitions, as with contract and with mutual and individual behaviors, all the combinations and generalizations of predicates and individuals can be carried out (such as κ(FG)-for-H[a] which was generalized as we went, for example, from SOC 1–4 to SOC 5 and 6).

6

Organizations

THE notion that the organization is fundamental to the study of social behavior is gaining increasing acceptance. In the preface to his work *Complex Organizations: A Critical Essay,* Perrow states:

> Twenty-five years ago the following statement would have been considered preposterous: all important social processes either have their origin in formal organizations or are strongly mediated by them; the study of organizations must be at the core of all social science. Today the first part of the statement is generally accepted, and I expect that within two decades the second part will also be accepted. [56: vii]

It is a relatively easy matter to cite examples of organizations. The term *organization* can refer to international agencies (such as the United Nations, the World Bank, NATO, etc.), governments, quasi-governmental regulatory agencies (such as stock exchanges, central banks, and standard-setting agencies), business firms, schools, charitable institutions, social clubs, professional associations, churches, families, and so on. Virtually all ongoing, regular social behavior (as distinguished from occasional, temporarily established social interactions) can be seen as manifesting itself within, or with reference to, organizations. Even so, no single definition of *organization* has been widely agreed upon; indeed, a definition of the term is not easy to find in most sociological, political-theoretic, or economic treatises. A sampling of definitional statements follows:

Organization . . . 1.c. *concr.*: An organized structure, body or being; an organism. . . . 2.c. *concr.*: An organized body, system or society. [52: v. 1, 2008]

A social relationship which is either closed or limits the admission of outsiders will be called an organization when its regulations are enforced by specific individuals: a chief and, possibly, an administrative staff, which normally also has representative powers. The incumbency of a policy-making position or participation in the functions of the staff constitute "executive powers." These may be appropriated, or they may be assigned, in accordance with the regulations of the organization, to specific persons or to individuals selected on the basis of specific characteristics or procedures. "Organized action" is (a) either the staff's action, which is legitimated by its executive or representative powers and oriented to realizing the organization's order, or (b) the members' action as directed by the staff.

An organization may be (a) autonomous or heteronomous, (b) autocephalous or heterocephalous. Autonomy means that the order governing the organization has been established by its own members on their own authority, regardless of how this has taken place in other respects. In the case of heteronomy, it has been imposed by an outside agency. Autocephaly means that the chief and his staff are selected according to the autonomous order of the organization itself, not, as in the case of heterocephaly, that they are appointed by outsiders. [69: 48–50]

Organization is a pattern of solidarity and cooperation. [35: 31]

An organization is a . . . system of action of a plurality of individuals, membership in which is defined by contractual commitments to given kinds and levels of performance (i.e., commitments to contribute to the organization function or goal and to perform agreed services to that end) . . . [55: 113]

A formal organization may be regarded as a group or cooperative system, with the following characteristics:

i. An accepted pattern of purposes . . . [At one extreme this pattern may consist of widespread dedication to common goals. At the other extreme, it may reflect *quid pro quo* bargains which give different returns to different members as rewards for their cooperation.]

ii. A sense of identification or belonging . . . [This sense of identification is heightened by the felt distinction between "in-group" and "out-group."]

iii. Continuity of interaction. The members of an organization interact with each other with some minimum degree of regularity and continuity. Members leave an organization by falling below the required minimum—as when a factory worker does not appear on the job any more, or when a union member stops paying dues.

iv. Differentiation of function. The activities of members of organizations are based upon some minimum amount of formal differentiation of roles. In small organizations the differentiation may be rudimentary. In larger organizations it becomes elaborate.

v. Conscious integration. The divided parts of an organization are held together not only by spontaneous cooperation but also by the conscious efforts of certain members responsible for bringing or holding them together. These, of course, are the administrators themselves, who bring people together for the formulation and achievement of an organization's purposes. [27: 41–42, 52–53]

The following characteristics of organizations are given in another current standard work:

Organizations are, of course, hierarchical in the sense that they are comprised of smaller units such as individuals and groups. [57: 17]

Organizations are, in many instances, physical entities. They have offices, buildings, factories, furniture, and some degree of physical dispersion or concentration. [57: 260]

In addition to their physical properties, organizations consist of patterned, repeated interactions among social actors. [57: 271]

[Organizations] are demographic entities characterized by demographic processes. Demography refers to the composition, in terms of basic attributes such as age, sex, educational level, length of service or residence, race, and so forth, of the social entity under study. [57: 277]

But beyond these descriptive statements, there is no formal definition of organization to be found in the book.

Our sampling indicates that the literature is rife with loosely formulated, incomplete, and vague discussions of the notion of organization; what we lack is a clear definition of the concept. In this chapter we discuss some of the problems that are encountered in attempting to construct formal definitions in this area.

The Traditional View of Organizations

March and Simon begin their landmark survey of organization theory as follows:

> It is easier, and probably more useful, to give examples of formal organizations than to define the term. The United States Steel Corporation is a formal organization; so is the Red Cross, the corner grocery store, the New York State Highway Department. The latter organization is, of course, part of a larger one—the New York State Government. But for present purposes we need not trouble ourselves about the precise boundaries to be drawn around an organization or the exact distinction between an "organization" and a "nonorganization." We are dealing with empirical phenomena, and the world has an uncomfortable way of not permitting itself to be fitted into clean classifications. [41: 1]

Note that in this paragraph the authors express a much less sanguine view of the nomological approach than they (especially Simon) do elsewhere. Certainly their position is quite different from the one taken in this lexicon. But of particular interest is the authors' assessment, in 1958, of the definitional status of the very notion of organization.[1] Moreover, the authors go on to develop a propositional inventory of organization theories structured in three groupings:

1. Propositions assuming that organization members . . . are primarily *passive instruments*.
2. Propositions assuming that members bring to their organizations *attitudes, values* and *goals:* that they have to be motivated or in-

---

1. In this respect there is no significant difference between the organization theory literature of today and that of 1958.

duced to participate in the system of organizational behavior: that there is incomplete parallelism between their personal goals and organization goals, and that . . . goal conflicts . . . make power phenomena, attitudes and morale internally important . . .

3. Propositions assuming that organization members are decision makers . . . and that perception . . . is . . . central to the explanation of behavior in organizations. [41: 8]

Propositions of the first sort are characteristic of the *structural approach* to organization theory (e.g., the scientific management theories of F. W. Taylor and Max Weber's theory of bureaucracy). Those of the second sort are characteristic of the *motivational approach* (e.g., the Hawthorne studies and the Michigan group dynamics research). Those of the third variety are characteristic of the *decision-making approach* (e.g., management science and organizational decision-making studies). Of special interest are the critical concepts in the above quotation, including those that March and Simon italicized and others as well, some of which are implicit in their language: features of organization structure, attitudes, values, goals, organizational goals, personal goals, decision, decision maker, perception, organization member, behavior, conflict, cooperation, and organization itself.

These concepts form a central core of ideas represented in all organization theories. Although some of these concepts have been defined in earlier chapters, the remainder must also be defined if we are to deal with organizations in this constructional system.

Extensions of the Traditional View

The noun *organization* has been widely used in three ways. The first, which is outside our immediate purpose, refers to the act or process of being organized, as in the statement: "Organization of an effective research group is a very difficult task."

Another sense in which the noun *organization* is used is as a plurality of human beings—or of psychological individuals, to use the terms of this lexicon—sharing goals and commitments in some way or another, and working together so as to attain them. Most large organizations, including business firms, large voluntary organizations, and governments, are of this type, as are smaller organizations such as households.

Finally, there is the conception of the organization as a machine. In this view of the organization there may be—indeed, there probably are—human beings involved, but for practical purposes most of them are not psychological individuals. That is, there is a virtual absence of individual autonomy, with, perhaps, the exception of the highest-level controllers of the organization. Athletic teams that rely on intricately coordinated plans, such as football teams, come to mind as an example, while other athletic teams, such as baseball, basketball, hockey, and soccer teams, allow for more individual autonomy.

The second and third views of organization may be thought of as end points of a continuum along which real organizations are distributed. The closer the organization is to the "machine" end of the continuum, the more "authoritarian" the organization is, while the closer the organization is to the "plurality of human beings" end, the more "democratic" the organization is.

It seems reasonable to think of an organization as a plurality of psychological individuals (i.e., a group) divided into subgroups that are functionally distinct (i.e., they perform unique functions within the organization). The memberships of these subgroups are not necessarily nonoverlapping. That is, an individual can belong to more than one subgroup—indeed, the memberships of two distinct subgroups could be identical—although neither of these circumstances is necessary. Each subgroup has a unique goal or set of goals. In addition, the attainment of these goals is instrumental (conducive) to the attainment of the organization's goal or goals. This means, then, that efforts to construct a definition of organization should focus on the following concerns: (1) goals of the subgroups and of the organization; (2) roles performed by members at all levels of the organization; (3) structure of relations between roles, between functional subgroups, and so on; and (4) incumbencies (i.e., role assignments to specific individuals).

Constructing Organization Definitions

Preliminaries

At various stages in this project, attempts were made to construct a set of definitions dealing with organization theory. None of these attempts has been entirely satisfactory, given the problems mentioned previously. But as a result of these efforts it is possible to sketch at least the outlines of a definition of organization.

An organization is a group whose membership is divided into at least two proper subsets each of which is an organization-component. Each organization-component has its own goal or goals. Each member of the organization-component has, or supports, the organization-component's goal(s). Pursuit of its goals by the organization-component somehow entails that members of the organization-component be in pursuit of those goals as well. Pursuit of its goals by an organization-component conduces to attainment of the organization's goals.

Each of the psychological individuals who make up the group that is the organization is a member of the organization. Moreover, each member of the organization is also a member of at least one organization-component, and no member of any organization-component is not also a member of the organization. Each organization-component is a proper subset of the organization in the sense that no organization-component's membership is identical with the organization's membership, which is to say that for each organization-component there is at least one member of the organization who is not a member of the organization-component.

An Example

Consider a number of psychological individuals who are all employed by a business firm. These persons make up a group. The firm, which is the organization, is set up with four functional subdivisions that are its organization-components: Manufacturing, Sales, Accounting and Finance, and Top Management. Top Management consists of the president and vice-president of the firm, their support staffs (staff specialists, product designers, secretaries, computer programmers and operators, etc.), and the heads of the other three organization-components. Each of the other organization-components consists of the head of the organization-component and the assistant chief of the component, plus their support staffs, plus the operating personnel of the organization-component. In Manufacturing, the operating personnel are the production-line workers and supervisors, maintenance workers, computer programmers and operators, etc. In Sales, the operating personnel are the sales staff plus their support staff, including computer programmers and operators. In Accounting and Finance, the operating personnel are the accountants, comptrollers, computer programmers and operators, and data-recording personnel, plus support staff. Note that there are computer programmers and operators in each organization-component. Some of these people, as well as some others, might serve in more than one organization-component.

Each organization-component has its own goals. Manufacturing's goal is to produce, at minimum cost, the product determined by Top Management in amounts determined by Top Management and with availability at times determined by Top Management. Sales' goals are to sell amounts of the product that fall into a range determined by Top Management so that the firm's inventory remains at an appropriate level, to sell product at prices and financial terms satisfactory to Top Management, and to ensure timely delivery and appropriate customer service. The goals of Accounting and Finance are to maintain records that allow for reliable, timely, and useful financial control at levels and in manners determined by national accounting and comptrollership associations, the IRS, and by Top Management. Top Management's goals are to determine product design, level of production, price, performance levels, and so on, for the operating components. The organization's goals are to maintain profit at satisfactory levels such that the organization can continue to operate successfully in the foreseeable future.

Goals

The example just given clearly demonstrates that satisfactory attainment of organization-component goals conduces to attainment of organization goals. When properly established, the set of organization-component goals should be necessary and sufficient for the attainment of organization goals, as long as external conditions are understood by the organization.

In constructing definitions related to organization theory, we need to clarify the concept of *goal*. In fact, we already have in hand something resembling that concept. Consider the functional predicate relation that we have been using: "K(FG)-for-H[b]." In this expression "H[b]," which is read "*b* has H," is the state of affairs that is the object of the functional predicate K(FG). That is to say, a K(FG) action is taken in order that *b* have H. Clearly, then, "H[b]" seems to be some sort of goal. It is an extremely specific goal—it specifies which individual will have which predicate (*b* will have H). In contrast, the sorts of goals that the organization and organization-components have are really collections of goals, or more general states of affairs all of which could be characterized as individuals having H-like predicates. One of the problems that must be faced in dealing with organizations is the generalization of whatever appears in the functional predicate notation as the desired state of affairs. One possibility is to simplify that notation by replacing "H[b]" with "*p*," where "*p*" is a statement describing the state of affairs that is the object of the K(FG) behavior. That does not completely solve the problem of generalization. But it does suggest that one could use a locution such as "the K(FG)-for-*p* psychological individual *y* has a θ-goal in τ." Here "θ-goal" would refer to any of a number of states of affairs that have certain characteristics in common, and "*p*" describes one of those states of affairs.

With this locution we must distinguish between the character of "*p*" and that of θ. Statement "*p*" describes the predicateness of individual *b* (does *b* have some predicate, say, H?). On the other hand, "θ" is itself a predicate and is the goal of someone whose goal is "*p*." To define "the K(FG)-for-*p* psychological individual *y* has a θ-goal in τ," we would say that at the time the psychological individual has the goal he does not have "θ," has not yet attained that state. Thus, so long as he does not have "θ," he is a K(FG)-for-*p* psychological individual. But once he does have "θ," he is no longer a K(FG)-for-*p* psychological individual. However, this still leads to two sorts of difficulties. One is coincidence. That is, suppose that as you attain your goal the sun sets, though that was not your goal. Still, it is difficult to avoid having that seem to have been your goal. The second problem arises because other things besides attainment of your goal, such as your death or a change in your attitude, might end your being a psychological individual for that "*p*."

Other difficulties arise in attempting to string goals of organization-components together so that they are related correctly to goals of the organization. Still another problem emerges in describing the time at which the goals are to be in effect. Are they to be at some specific interval in the future, at any (finite) interval in the future, or forever, after some future time? To overcome these difficulties, the notion of goals, particularly as they relate to organizations, requires additional work.

Membership and Structure

We need to distinguish an organization member who is effective in the attainment of some organization or organization-component goal from a member who is ineffective or nonfunctional. In addition, we need to distinguish someone who is purposely ineffective or even counterproductive (we might call the latter a "mole" in the organization) from someone who strives (and sometimes succeeds) to be effective. And we must distinguish between competent and incompetent members who are not moles. Incompetent nonmoles might be called "dupes." So, organization members could be of three sorts: genuine members, moles, and dupes.

Members whose roles are extremely constrained, that is, whose responsibilities are confined to following orders with no exercise of discretion, should be distinguished from members who can exercise discretion. The former might be called "cogs" in the organization. But it is important to define carefully the notion of discretion (or its absence).

Once these problems are solved, it should not be difficult to bring the notions of cooperation, conflict, and teleological independence, as well as the varieties of agreement, contract, etc., developed on the level of the individual in chapter 5, into use in discussing organizations. But until these problems are solved, we can do nothing with the stable patterns of interaction among individuals that characterize organizations. And there is no doubt that it is in such interaction patterns that much of the most important social behavior takes place.

7

Implications for Social Science Theories

WE have constructed 126 definitions that cover a range of concepts: individual decision, cooperative behavior, conflicting behavior, teleologically independent behavior, agreement, contract, payment, and others. We have shown that within these general domains the construction of additional definitions as they are needed does not present serious problems. Moreover, some preliminaries have been laid out for tackling the problems involved in constructing a set of definitions related to organization theory.

This lexicon is offered as an example of a definitional system that could be useful in testing, examining, and eventually formulating social science theories. It is not proposed as the only true and correct constructional system of definitions for the social sciences—there is surely a multitude of alternative systems, based on different sets of primitives, employing different logical commitments, and using different strategies for interrelating phenomenal fields of social behavior. Thus, in this fundamental respect this lexicon is not part of, nor an extension of, the logical positivist program. If this system proves to be workable and effective, the important results will be that the effectiveness of a general strategy for dealing with social science theories will have been demonstrated and that the strategy may come into widespread use. Much less important would be the demonstration that *this* system has been useful.

In this final chapter we discuss three basic issues. First, how may a system of this sort be used? That is, what types of problems related to social science theories can this system help to solve? Second, what particular applications appear immediately promising? In other words, what theories or theoretical problems might first be attacked with this set of tools? Third, what significant philosophical and procedural problems must be faced if this system is to be widely accepted?

The Uses of a Constructional Definitional System

The Fundamental Logical Commitment

A constructional definitional system is first and foremost a logical system. The primary worth of such a system is that it introduces the powers of formal logic into theoretical discourse at the most fundamental levels. The informed user of a constructional system will insist that all terms used in the body of relevant theory be drawn from the constructional system itself and from its logical and mathematical antecedents. That is, as it becomes necessary to introduce additional concepts they should be formulated within the constructional system, not simply appended from outside. Because of this, and because of the way in which a constructional system is built, all aspects of the theoretical discourse above the level of the choice of primitive terms and axioms are infused with and exposed to the analytical mechanism of formal logic. Indeed, the value of a constructional definitional system is that it allows us to take advantage of this analytical mechanism.

Having said this, we might next ask exactly what is implied by the introduction of formal logic into theoretical discourse. A constructional definitional system allows us to examine the logical consistency of existing scientific theories, to generate new theorems in existing scientific theories, and to express wholly new scientific theories. Before examining these implications in greater detail, we must consider how logical manipulations of components of these theories can be practically carried out. A cursory examination of some of the formal definitions in appendices D, F, and H suggests that paper-and-pencil manipulation of expressions containing these defined terms, with symbols denoting numbers of distinct predicates and individuals embedded in them, would be a horrifyingly complex task. The opportunity for error in such manipulation seems astronomical. If our definitional system merely allows us to trade intuition for infinitely burdensome detail, we have probably gained nothing at all.

However, in recent years a number of technological developments hold out the promise of our being able to deal with this problem mechanically. There is first the availability of computing power that was undreamed of in the mid-1950s and early 1960s, as well as the development of logic-processing software packages including LISP, LOGLISP, other LISP-based languages, PROLOG, and, most recently, the more powerful logical analysis packages such as ITP and OTTER. These technologies enable us to load the definitions of a theory (which in all likelihood means an augmented set of the definitions presented in this book), plus its axioms and theorems, into the memory of a computer that has access to a logic-processor, and then to carry out a series of examinations, searches, and implication checks. There are some limitations to the powers of logic-processors, but most of the burdensome computational work can be done electronically.

Consistency of Scientific Theories

Any putative scientific theory in the social sciences (or in any other body of science) should be capable of logical assessment. That is, for each theory we want to know the following: Is the theory a consistent set of statements? What are its axioms, or the set of logically independent statements from which logically follow the balance of the statements of the theory? Are there some fundamental inconsistencies buried in the theory? Are the putative theorems of the theory demonstrably implied by the axioms?

Such scrutiny is possible once the theory is recast so that all its terms are placed within the constructional system. This involves assigning definitions that are within the constructional system to all terms used in the theory, or constructing new definitions that are within the system and that are expressed as definitions of terms used in the theory.

It is at this point that conflict may arise between the proponents of the preconstructional theory and the constructionalists. If the conflict is limited to differences of opinion regarding definitional strategy, the matter might be relatively easy to resolve. If, for example, two proposals were put forward for defining a particular term, or range or group of terms, *within the confines of the instant definitional system,* both proposals could be pursued and their implications explored. However, if the conflict is based on irresolvable differences regarding the choice of primitive terms, then it would be necessary to erect an entirely new constructional system. This could be done but would be quite time consuming. Finally, the conflict might be over the inherent feasibility of devising a set of meaningful definitions within a constructional system. In this case we have two parties, one of which is a constructionalist and the other of which insists that, at least for the theory under consideration, constructionalism can be of no use. As a constructionalist I would regret that partisans of the theory took the latter position, but nevertheless I would carefully attempt to apply an appropriate constructional system to the theory.

Once the terms of the theory have been recast according to the constructional definitional system, the analytical mechanism of formal logic can be applied to it. As we saw in chapter 1, a scientific theory is a collection of two sorts of statements. The first are the axioms, a group of logically independent statements that are hypothesized of the situation being examined. The second are the theorems, the statements that are logically implied by the axioms.

Many bodies of statements have been offered as social science theories, but most often their components have not been clearly identified nor has their logical character been examined. Our concern now is to see whether a particular body of statements is indeed a theory. Are any of the statements identified as the theory's axioms? Are they truly logically independent? If the answer to either of these questions is no, can we identify a set of the theory's statements that would serve as axioms? Whatever set of axioms we find in our hands, are any of the balance of the statements of the theory implied by them? If some are not, what is their theoretical status, and what is their provenance in the theory? That is, how did they come to be introduced into the theory?

Such questions can be answered once the theory is stated in terms of a constructional definitional system. The result of this examination can be viewed as a logical "report card" for the particular theory, one that provides indications of how the logical failings might be remedied or an assessment of the difficulty of remedying them.

By itself such a report card would be of limited interest. But real advantages emerge if the embracing constructional system clearly connects any statements involving its definitions with empirical observations. Then the report card becomes a plan for formal and systematic empirical testing of the theory.

Hidden Content of Existing Theories

By exploiting the logical power of the reformulated theory it should be possible to generate many further logically implied statements (theorems) beyond those present in the theory. Perhaps the vast majority of these will be of no great scientific interest. But some deductions from the axioms might emerge that are not obvious at first glance but that are possibly clearer, more interesting, and more powerful applications of the theory.

Thus, the definitional system might serve as a testing ground for infant theories in the social sciences. And it would in all likelihood aid in the further formalization and development of such theories. Empirical testability of additional theorems would be dependent on the character of the constructional system.

New Theories

In addition to operating on previously developed theories in the social sciences, it also makes sense to express a body of theoretical statements *ab initio* using the terms of this lexicon. The theorist would start from scratch in developing a theory based on this constructional system instead of translating, and then further developing, extant theories in terms of this definitional scheme. Thus, the social science theorist would work in these terms as theoretical physicists do in theirs, rather than according to personal proclivities or tastes as occurred in the natural sciences before Newton and is too often the case in the social sciences now. All the advantages delineated above would be afforded to the theorist from the outset. In addition, the lateral connectibility, as well as the local reducibility, of this new theory to existing theories, and to those that might follow, would be much clearer if the theories had a common definitional basis. The implications of this approach are clear for the development of an articulated body of scientific statements, and the advantages immense.

Some Potential Applications

Parsonian Theory

When the Parsonian corpus began to appear in the early 1950s, it was heralded as a framework for theorizing in the social sciences. I think it fair to describe much of the Parsonian corpus as a prelogical theoretical framework, and there are portions that seem to lend themselves especially to constructional treatment [53], [54], and [55]. Of particular interest for its interdisciplinary character, linking sociology and economics, is the work by Parsons and Smelser [55]. This work appears to be a prime candidate for direct, slightly augmented restatement in terms of the present constructional system. Successful treatment of this sort might lead to an enrichment of the institutionalist view in economics, allowing institutions direct entry into economic theories.

Post-Keynesian Economics

During the past ten to fifteen years a body of macroeconomic literature devoted to post-Keynesian economics has developed [13], [18], [32], [33], [43], [44], and [45]. Characteristic of the post-Keynesian approach is a greater concern with economic institutions than is found in mainstream macroeconomics. Moreover, because this approach is a less mathematical treatment of macroeconomics, the logic of post-Keynesian theorizing has been generally less tight and formal. Augmentation of this lexicon's constructional system should render it useful for treating some aspects of post-Keynesian economics. Given the disarray in which macroeconomics has found itself during the past decade and a half, useful results might emerge from this application.

Ethnocentrism

LeVine and Campbell present another instance of a prelogical theoretical system [37, esp. chapters 3 and 8]. Some preliminary work has been done in restating the ethnocentrism framework in terms of the constructional system presented in this lexicon. This application presents fewer interdisciplinary possibilities than do the two previous applications; nevertheless, it is of great interest.

Collective Choice Theory

Literature on the theory of social choice has burgeoned since the appearance in 1951 of Arrow's seminal work [1]. Although many fascinating and paradoxical results have been reported, it seems likely that enriching the notions of preference and of roles played by the holders of preferences will open up other interesting questions. Combining the constructional approach with the computational treatment of these issues may be a promising line of investigation.

Revolution and Coup d'état

As we saw in chapter 6, an organization can be viewed as a group of individuals divided into subgroups that are functionally distinct (i.e., they perform unique functions within the organization). Each subgroup has its own goal or set of goals. Moreover, attainment of the subgroup's goals is instrumental to the attainment of the organization's goals. Thus, the definition of *organization* is concerned with the following: (1) goals of the subgroups and of the organization; (2) roles performed by members at all levels of the organization; (3) structure of relations between roles and between functional subgroups, etc.; and (4) incumbencies (i.e., role assignments to particular individuals).

A *reorganization* can be thought of as any sort of change in any of these four aspects of the organization. Depending on which aspects change, there are at least four major types of reorganization. Since a government is a type of organization, these comments could apply to governments as well as to other organizations. If the reorganization of a government takes place without the consent of those whose agreement is required by law, the reorganization could be spoken of as a *revolution*. There are, then, at least four types of revolutions. If incumbencies alone change, a *coup d'état* has occurred. If incumbencies and structure of relations change, a *structural revolution* has taken place. If incumbencies, structure of relations, and roles change, the revolution is even more substantial. If goals as well as incumbencies, structure of relations, and roles change, then what has occurred is a true *social revolution*. A goal-change revolution is likely to entail role, structure, and incumbency change. A role-change revolution may not entail goal change, but it probably involves structure and incumbency change. A structure-change revolution may not entail change in roles and goals, but it probably involves change in incumbency. A coup d'état, however, probably does not go beyond incumbency change. Detailed examination and classification of this set of phenomena would surely be facilitated by the use of a constructional definitional system.

An Earlier Lexicon

Lasswell and Kaplan's attempt to devise a lexicon for political theory [35] might lend itself to formalization by means of this constructional system. This effort would lead to a substantial expansion of the list of formally defined terms concerned with power and social structure. Thus, a significant capital asset would be built for the social sciences.

Behavioral Theory of the Firm

Cyert and March's imaginative treatment of the business firm as an organization in the Simonian tradition [12] provides the basis for another interesting application. This approach does not deal with the firm in the extremely abstract fashion of neoclassical theory, which depicts the firm as a sealed black box absorbing factors of production and emitting products and profits (or losses). Instead the behavioral approach takes into account the firm's internal structure, local internal motivations and behaviors, and the details of interfirm and other external relations. Cyert and March have presented a number of theories in the form of computer-simulation models. Testing of such models is subject to severe limitations and is rather primitive. But if the methods developed in this lexicon are applied, the models might be subjected to real logical analysis, thereby bringing institutionalist and theoretical economics into more intimate contact.

Problems

Two basic problems have appeared regarding the application of this constructional definitional system to social science theories. One is the set of philosophical questions that have to do with the very feasibility of this sort of system. The other has to do with procedural difficulties that must be overcome if the system is to gain widespread acceptance.

Philosophical Questions

Among those who raise questions about the feasibility of applying the constructional definitional system are those philosophers who persist in seeing this enterprise as a part of the logical positivist program. For these people the problems of the social scientist are not distinguishable from those of other scientists. Their point of view might be summarized as follows: Axiomatic treatments in science are interesting but extraordinarily difficult to carry out, so why undertake them unless they are part of the logical positivist program, or something like it that leads to massive reduction and unification? These critics—who are philosophers, not scientists—view science as something that is perfectible and that should be perfected now. For the scientist, not only is science *not* perfectible, but attempts to perfect it only detract from the energy that should be devoted to carrying it on, however imperfect it continues to be. Philosophers tend not to think in terms of cutting Gordian knots, while how to cut Gordian knots most efficiently is constantly on the mind of the active scientist. Mopping-up operations to eliminate the lacunae, and the messiness, can be done later.

Another type of philosophical objection goes something like this: How can we justify attempts to formalize and empiricize our understanding of all sorts of concepts while at the same time we tolerate such a troublesome primitive term as P5, "individuals that have F believe that p"? It is pointed out that P5 is not neat, that it involves imputation of internal (mental) states, and that everything in this system that is not social physics depends on it. My response is that until we can find some better way of handling belief and perception, our only alternative to not trying at all is to go forward with the best available definitions.

Procedural Problems

Procedural problems center on two issues. First, there is the problem of specifying predicates, especially predicates that stand in functional relation to one another as in K(FG)-for-H[a] or K(FG)-for-p. Second, there is the problem of specifying individuals that will be useful in formulating expressions about particular empirical situations. Both problems will have to be dealt with on an ad hoc basis, and an understanding of effective procedures for specifying predicates and individuals will have to be gained through trial and error and experience.

With the appearance of this lexicon, social scientists should find that a new and powerful tool has become available, one that will aid in the formulation, development, and logical analysis of social science theories. If this assessment is correct, the social sciences will be in a better position to become nomological sciences, with all the good and evil consequences, both social and scientific, that may flow from such a development.

Appendices

Appendix A. Notation

THE notational conventions used in formal expressions (displayed definitions and "readings" of terms as well as formal logical notation) are spelled out below. Note that the formal logical notation found in appendices D, F, and H has been devised to accommodate easy loading of the lexicon into a computer.[1]

1. Primitive terms are set in boldface type in all formal expressions. Boldface is not used for any other symbols. Thus:

    overlaps(x,y)

2. In formal expressions, predicate variables are designated by double-width uppercase letters. The underscore "_" rather than the hyphen is used in formal logical notation (but only in formal logical nota-

---

1. When this lexicon is being applied on a computer, the notation will need further adaptation to meet the demands of particular software programs. This adaptation takes four general forms: First, logical operators are expressed in special ways. For example, in OTTER 1.0 the universal quantifier is expressed as "(all x)" followed by the formula to which it applies. Second, there are specific requirements about the use of parentheses and blank spaces that vary from software package to software package. In written logical forms there are no such requirements. Third, these programs usually have strict requirements regarding the use of ellipses. OTTER 1.0 does not allow for such forms as "1, . . . , *n*." This means, then, that expressions must be fully constructed, not implied by ellipsis. Finally, these programs usually do not allow the use of square brackets, braces, or semicolons.

tion) to connect bits of words in naming formal predicates to avoid confusion with the minus sign. Thus:

K, **F**, **G**, or **H** as in
"FUNC_PRED_**K**(**FG**)_for_**H**[a](**K**{**F**,**G**,**H**[a]})"

3. In formal expressions individuals are designated by lowercase roman letters. Thus:

a, b, c, . . . , w, x, y, z

In textual commentary individuals and other variables are set in lowercase italic letters.

4. An individual has predicates. This is indicated in formal expressions by the predicate letter followed by the individual letter or other designator enclosed in square brackets. In some cases there are rather complex designators for individuals that have a predicate. But these will always follow the predicate letter and will be enclosed in square brackets. Square brackets are used in no other way. Thus:

H[a] as in
"FUNC_PRED_**K**(**FG**)_for_**H**[a](**K**{**F**,**G**,**H**[a]})"

5. A functional predicate may be so described, or in formal expressions it may be written as the predicate letter followed by braces enclosing a list of the predicates that make up the function. The last element in the list will be the individual in square brackets; the goal of the functional predicate is to attach the list of predicates to the individual. Braces will be used in no other way. Thus:

K{**F**,**G**,**H**[a]} as in
"FUNC_PRED_**K**(**FG**)_for_**H**[a](**K**{**F**,**G**,**H**[a]})"

Finally, since an individual may have this functional predicate, the functional predicate may be followed by the symbol for an individual enclosed in its own square brackets. In the following example

"FUNC_BEH_**K**(**FG**)_for_**H**[a](x,**K**{**F**,**G**,**H**[a]} [x];τ)"

note the appearance of x in square brackets toward the end of the expression. This means that x has the predicate $\mathbf{K}\{\mathbf{F},\mathbf{G},\mathbf{H}[a]\}$.

6. The logical notation used is essentially the Peano-Russell notation but with a few differences to accommodate readers of this work who are not, at the outset, thoroughly familiar with symbolic logic. I have, for example, chosen for the universal quantifier one connective symbol that is not found, in the exact form in which I use it, in any system of logical notation. The symbol is ordinarily (x) or, in set-theoretic notation, ∀. We will use (∀), as in (∀x). This notation is chosen because (x) is easily confused with ordinary functional notation and because the freestanding ∀ is not clearly identified as a quantifier. For similar reasons we use the ampersand, found in the Hilbert-Ackermann system, for conjunction, rather than the dot found in the Peano-Russell notation. With these exceptions, the formal logical notation of this lexicon is that of the Peano-Russell system. Thus:

Negation is indicated by $-$, as in "$-x$," which is read as *not x*.

Conjunction is indicated by &, as in "x & y," which is read as *x and y*.

Alternation is indicated by v, as in "x v y," which is read as *x or y*.

Implication is indicated by ⊃, as in "x ⊃ y," which is read as *if x then y*.

The biconditional is indicated by ≡, as in "x ≡ y," which is read as *x if and only if y*.

The universal quantifier is indicated by ∀, as in "(∀x)," which is read as *for any x* or *for all x*.

The existential quantifier is indicated by ∃, as in "(∃x)," which is read as *there is at least one x such that*.

The symbol l indicates discreteness or distinctness, as in "x l y," which is read as *x is distinct from y*.

The symbol l identifies the individual that has a particular predicate, as in "(l x)(father of z)," which is read as *the x that is the father of z*.

A time-interval is usually designated by the symbol τ.

7. One other deviation from standard notation is necessitated by the use of nominalist logic. Because predicate variables are not individual variables, they cannot be modified by the universal or existential quantifiers. Yet it would be convenient if they could be referred to in such fashion as to allow reference to all predicates, or to the availability of some predicate, satisfying certain conditions. This is done by underlining a predicate variable to indicate the analogue to the existential quantifier and by preceding it with an asterisk to indicate the analogue to the universal quantifier. Thus:

"**K**" would be read as *some predicate* **K**, while "*****K**" would be read as *all predicates* **K**.

8. Defined terms are themselves predicates. They are designated in the logical notation by a sequence of uppercase roman letters and underscore marks (no spaces) followed by arguments enclosed in even numbers of parentheses and pairs of braces or square brackets as described previously.

9. In appendixes D, F, and H, each definition is given first in its informal form, definiendum first, in quotes, followed by the symbol " = df." Then, in quotes, follows the definiens in informal form. The formal definitions follow the same order: definiendum in quotes, followed by " = df.," followed by the definiens in quotes. The definitions are given in groups, as follows:

Auxiliaries (AUX)
Decision terms (DEC)
Socioeconomic terms (SOC)

Appendix B. List of Primitives

P1 **overlaps**(x,y) may be read as *x overlaps y*

P2 **e_slice**(x,y) may be read as *x is an earlier time-slice than y*

P3 **morph_id**(x,y) may be read as *x is morphologically identical to y*

P4 **con**(x,p) may be read as *x conduces to p*

P5 **bel**(**F**,p) may be read as *individuals that have* **F** *believe that p*

P6 **index**(x,**F**) may be read as *x satisfies an index of* **F**

Appendix C. Auxiliary Terms:
Readings of Definientia

AUX 1   "x is part of y"

AUX 2   "x is identical to y"

AUX 3   "x is a time-slice"

AUX 4   "x is a time-interval"

AUX 5   "z is the sum of x and y"

AUX 6   "z is the difference of x and y (x minus y)"

AUX 7   "z is the product of x and y"

AUX 8   "x is the slice-part of y in time-slice z"

AUX 9   "x is the interval-part of y in time-interval τ"

AUX 10   "x and y are discrete slice-parts of z"

AUX 11   "x is an earlier-and-discrete time-interval relative to y"

AUX 12   "x and y are discrete interval-parts of z"

AUX 13   "τ' is a terminating time of time-interval τ"

AUX 14   "x is the fusion of the predicate '$\mathbf{F}$' "

AUX 15   "x satisfies an index of $\mathbf{F}$ in time-interval τ"

AUX 16   "on the grounds that he is an **F**, x believes, in time-interval τ, that p"

AUX 17   "on the grounds that he is **F**-able, x believes, in time-interval τ, that p"

AUX 18   "x believes, in time-interval τ, that p"

AUX 19   "x has veridical belief, in time-interval τ, that p"

AUX 20   "x has nonveridical belief, in time-interval τ, that p"

AUX 21   "x perceives, in time-interval τ, that p"

AUX 22   "x veridically perceives, in time-interval τ, that p"

AUX 23   "x nonveridically perceives, in time-interval τ, that p"

AUX 24   "**F** is a universal predicate"

AUX 25   "**F** is a one-place morphological predicate"

AUX 26   "x undergoes change with respect to predicate **F** in time-interval τ"

AUX 27   "x undergoes morphological change with respect to predicate **F** in time-interval τ"

AUX 28   "x undergoes change in time-interval τ"

AUX 29   "x undergoes morphological change in time-interval τ"

AUX 30   "**K** is a behavioral predicate"

AUX 31   "x exhibits **K**-behavior in time-interval τ"

AUX 32   "x exhibits behavior in time-interval τ"

AUX 33   "**K** is a behavioral predicate with respect to **F**-change"

AUX 34   "x exhibits morphological **K**-behavior in time-interval τ"

AUX 35   "x exhibits morphological behavior in time-interval τ"

AUX 36   "x is an event at time τ"

AUX 37   "x is an event"

AUX 38   "person x expects, in time-interval τ, that event y will occur in time-interval τ'"

AUX 39   "person x plans, in time-interval τ, that x exhibits **B**-behavior in time-interval τ'"

AUX 40   "persons x and y mutually plan, in time-interval τ, that x will exhibit **B**-behavior in time-interval τ' *and* y will exhibit **B'**-behavior in time-interval τ''"

Appendix D. Auxiliary Terms: Formal Definitions

AUX 1   "x is part of y" = df.
        "everything that overlaps x overlaps y"
          "PART(x,y)" = df.
          "$(\forall z)$(**overlaps**$(z,x) \supset$ **overlaps**$(z,y))$"

AUX 2   "x is identical to y" = df.
        "x is part of y *and* y is part of x"
          "IDENT(x,y)" = df.
          "PART(x,y) & PART(y,x)"

AUX 3   "x is a time-slice" = df.
        "there is something that is an earlier time-slice than x"
          "SLICE(x)" = df.
          "$(\exists y)$(**e_slice**$(y,x))$"

AUX 4   "x is a time-interval" = df.
        Conjunct 1. "every time-slice that overlaps x is part of x *and*
        Conjunct 2. there are at least two distinct time-slices that are parts
                of x *and*
        Conjunct 3. given any two time-slices that are parts of x, every
                time-slice later than the earlier of these *and* earlier
                than the later of them is also part of x *and*
        Conjunct 4. there are time-slices earlier than any time-slice that is
                part of x *and* there are time-slices later than any time-
                slice that is part of x"

"INTVL(x)" = df.

"(∀y)(SLICE(y) & **overlaps**(y,x)⊃PART(y,x)) &
(∃z)(∃z′)(SLICE(z) & SLICE(z′) & − IDENT(z,z′) &
PART(z,x) & PART(z′,x)) & (∀z)(∀z′)(SLICE(z) &
SLICE(z′) & PART(z,x) & PART(z′,x) &
e_slice(z,z′)⊃(∀z″)(SLICE(z″) & **e_slice**(z,z″) &
e_slice(z″,z′)⊃PART(z″,x)) & (∀z)(SLICE(z) &
PART (z,x)⊃(∃w)(SLICE(w) & − PART(w,x) &
e_slice(w,z)) & (∃w′)(SLICE(w′) & − PART(w′,x) &
e_slice(z,w′))"

AUX 5   "z is the sum of x and y" = df.
"w is part of z *if and only if* w is part of x *or* w is part of y"
"SUM(z,x,y)" = df.
"(ιz)(∀w)(PART(w,z)≡(PART(w,x) ∨ PART(w,y)))"

AUX 6   "z is the difference of x and y (x minus y)" = df.
"y is part of x *and* everything that overlaps z overlaps x *and* does
not overlap y"
"DIFF(z,x,y)" = df.
"PART(y,x) & (∀w)(**overlaps**(w,z)⊃**overlaps**(w,x) &
− **overlaps**(w,y))"

AUX 7   "z is the product of x and y" = df.
"if x overlaps y, then any w is part of z *if and only if* w is part of
x, *and if* x does not overlap y, *then* z is the sum of x and y"
"PROD(z,x,y)" = df.
"(ιz)(**overlaps**(x,y)⊃(∀w)(PART(w,z)≡PART(w,x) &
PART(w,y)) & (− **overlaps**(x,y)⊃SUM(z,x,y)))"

AUX 8   "x is the slice-part of y in time-slice z" = df.
"z is a time-slice *and* y overlaps z *and* x is the product of y and
z"
"SP(x,y,z)" = df.
"SLICE(z) & **overlaps**(y,z) & PROD(z,x,y)"

AUX 9   "x is the interval-part of y in time-interval τ" = df.
"τ is a time-interval *and* y overlaps τ *and* x is the product of y
and τ"
"IP(x,y,τ)" = df.
"INTVL(τ) & **overlaps**(y,τ) & PROD(x,y,τ)"

AUX 10   "x and y are discrete slice-parts of z" = df.
"x is the slice-part of z in some time-slice *and* y is the slice-part
of z in some different (distinct) time-slice"
"DSP(x,y,z)" = df.
"(∃w)(∃w')(SLICE(w) & SLICE(w') & −IDENT(w,w') &
SP(x,z,w) & SP(y,z,w'))"

AUX 11   "x is an earlier-and-discrete time-interval relative to y" = df.
"x and y are both time-intervals *and* every time-slice that is part
of x is earlier than any time-slice that is part of y"
"EDT(x,y)" = df.
"INTVL(x) & INTVL(y) & (∀s)(∀s')(SLICE(s) & SLICE(s')
& PART(s,x) & PART(s',y)⊃**e_slice**(s,s'))"

AUX 12   "x and y are discrete interval-parts of z" = df.
"there are two time-intervals, τ and τ', that are discrete from one
another, *and* x is the interval-part of z in one of them *and* y is the
interval-part of z in the other"
"DIP(x,y,z)" = df.
"(∃τ)(∃τ')(INTVL(τ) & INTVL(τ') & −**overlaps**(τ,τ') &
IP(x,z,τ) & IP(y,z,τ))"

AUX 13   "τ' is a terminating time of time-interval τ" = df.
"τ is an earlier-and-discrete time-interval relative to τ' *and* there
is no time-interval τ" such that τ" is an earlier-and-discrete time-
interval relative to τ' *and* τ is an earlier-and-discrete time-interval
relative to τ""
"TERM(τ',τ)" = df.
"EDT(τ,τ') & (∀τ")−(∃τ")(EDT(τ",τ') & EDT(τ,τ"))"

AUX 14   "x is the fusion of the predicate '**F**' " = df.
"everything that satisfies **F** is part of x, *and* everything that is
part of x overlaps something that satisfies **F**"
"FU(**F**,x)" = df.
"(∀y)(**F**[y]⊃PART(y,x)) & (∀z)(PART(z,x)⊃(∃w)(**F**[w] &
overlaps(z,w)))"

AUX 15   "x satisfies an index of **F** in time-interval τ" = df.
"the interval-part of x in time-interval τ satisfies an index of **F**"

"IX($\mathbf{F}$,x,τ)" = df.
"**index**((ιy)IP(y,x,τ),$\mathbf{F}$)"

AUX 16   "on the grounds that he is an $\mathbf{F}$, x believes, in time-interval τ, that p" = df.
"individuals that have $\mathbf{F}$ believe that p, *and* the interval-part of x in time-interval τ is an $\mathbf{F}$"
"O_BLF($\mathbf{F}$,p,x,τ)" = df.
"**bel**($\mathbf{F}$,p) & $\mathbf{F}$[(ιy)IP(y,x,τ)]"

AUX 17   "on the grounds that he is $\mathbf{F}$-able, x believes, in time-interval τ, that p" = df.
"on the grounds that he is an $\mathbf{F}$, x believes, in time-interval τ, that p; *or* individuals that have $\mathbf{F}$ believe that p *and* the interval-part of x in time-interval τ satisfies an index of $\mathbf{F}$"
"$\mathbf{F}$_BLF($\mathbf{F}$,p,x,τ)" = df.
"(O_BLF($\mathbf{F}$,p,x,τ)) $\vee$ ($\mathbf{F}$[(ιy)IP(y,x,τ)] & IX(O_BLF($\mathbf{F}$,p,x,τ)))"

AUX 18   "x believes, in time-interval τ, that p" = df.
"there is at least one predicate $\mathbf{F}$ such that on the grounds that x is $\mathbf{F}$-able, x believes, in time-interval τ, that p"
"BLF(p,x,τ)" = df.
"$\mathbf{F}$_BLF($\underline{\mathbf{F}}$,p,x,τ)"

AUX 19   "x has veridical belief, in time-interval τ, that p" = df.
" 'p' is true *and* x believes, in time-interval τ, that p"
"V_BLF(p,x,τ)" = df.
"p & BLF(p,x,τ)"

AUX 20   "x has nonveridical belief, in time-interval τ, that p" = df.
" 'p' is false *and* x believes, in time-interval τ, that p"
"NV_BLF(p,x,τ)" = df.
"$-$p & BLF(p,x,τ)"

AUX 21   "x perceives, in time-interval τ, that p" = df.
"x believes, in time-interval τ, that p"
"PRCV(p,x,τ)" = df.
"BLF(p,x,τ)"

AUX 22   "x veridically perceives, in time-interval τ, that p" = df.
"x has veridical belief, in time-interval τ, that p"

"V_PRCV(p,x,τ)" = df.
"V_BLF(p,x,τ)"

AUX 23   "x nonveridically perceives, in time-interval τ, that p" = df.
"x has nonveridical belief, in time-interval τ, that p"
  "NV_PRCV(p,x,τ)" = df.
  "NV_BLF(p,x,τ)"

AUX 24   "**F** is a universal predicate" = df.
"for all x, x is an **F**"
  "U(**F**)" = df.
  "($\forall$x)**F**[x]"

AUX 25   "**F** is a one-place morphological predicate" = df.
"**F** is not a universal predicate *and* whenever two things are morphologically identical one is an **F** *if and only if* the other is also"
  "MRF(**F**)" = df.
  "$-$U(**F**) & ($\forall$x)($\forall$y)(**morph_id**(x,y)$\supset$(**F**[x]$\equiv$**F**[y]))"

AUX 26   "x undergoes change with respect to predicate **F** in time-interval τ" = df.
"τ is a time-interval *and* there are two time-intervals y and z that are parts of τ such that the interval-part of x with respect to one of them is an **F** *and* the interval-part of x with respect to the other is not"
  "**F**_CHANGE(**F**,x,τ)" = df.
  "INTVL(τ) & ($\exists$y)($\exists$z)(PART(y,τ) & PART(z,τ) & DSP(y,z,x) & **F**[y] & $-$**F**[z])"

AUX 27   "x undergoes morphological change with respect to predicate **F** in time-interval τ" = df.
"**F** is a one-place morphological predicate *and* x undergoes change with respect to predicate **F** in time-interval τ"
  "MRF_**F**_CHANGE(**F**,x,τ)" = df.
  "MRF(**F**) & **F**_CHANGE(**F**,x,τ)"

AUX 28   "x undergoes change in time-interval τ" = df.
"there is at least one predicate **F** in the language such that **F**-change has occurred with respect to that predicate in time-interval τ"

"CH(x,τ)" = df.
"**F**_CHANGE(**F**,x,τ)"

AUX 29   "x undergoes morphological change in time-interval τ" = df.
"x undergoes morphological change with respect to some one-
place morphological predicate in time-interval τ"
"MRF_CH(x,τ)" = df.
"MRF_**F**_CHANGE(**F**,x,τ)"

AUX 30   "**K** is a behavioral predicate" = df.
"whenever anything satisfies **K** there is a time when it does so
and satisfies some predicate **F** that it does not satisfy at some
other time when it satisfies **K**"
"BEH_PRD(**K**)" = df.
"(∀x)(∀τ)(INTVL(τ) & **K**[(ιy)IP(y,x,τ)]⊃CH(x,τ))"

AUX 31   "x exhibits **K**-behavior in time-interval τ" = df.
"**K** is a behavioral predicate *and* τ is a time-interval *and* the
interval-part of x in τ is a **K**"
"**K**_BEH(**K**,x,τ)" = df.
"BEH_PRD(**K**) & INTVL(τ) & **K**[(ιy)IP(y,x,τ)]"

AUX 32   "x exhibits behavior in time-interval τ" = df.
"x exhibits **K**-behavior in time-interval τ with respect to some
behavioral predicate **K**"
"BEH(x,τ)" = df.
"**K**_BEH(**K̲**,x,τ)"

AUX 33   "**K** is a behavioral predicate with respect to **F**-change" = df.
"all and only those things that satisfy **K** during a given time-
interval undergo **F**-change during that time-interval"
"BEH_PRD_**F**_CHANGE(**K**,**F**)" = df.
"(∀x)(**K**[x]≡(∃y)(∃z)(DSP(y,z,x) & **F**[y] & − **F**[z]))"

AUX 34   "x exhibits morphological **K**-behavior in time-interval τ" = df.
"for some morphological predicate **F**, **K** is a behavioral
predicate with respect to **F**-change *and* x exhibits **K**-behavior in
time-interval τ"
"MRF_**K**_BEH(**K**,x,τ)" = df.
"MRF(**F̲**) & BEH_CHANGE(**K**,**F̲**) & **K**_BEH(**K**,x,τ)"

AUX 35   "x exhibits morphological behavior in time-interval τ" $=$ df.
"for some predicate **K**, x exhibits morphological **K**-behavior in time-interval τ"
"MRF_BEH(x,τ)" $=$ df.
"MRF_**K**_BEH(**K**,x,τ)"

AUX 36   "x is an event at time τ" $=$ df.
"some part of x behaves in time-interval τ"
"τ_EVNT(x,τ)" $=$ df.
"($\exists$z)(PART(z,x) & BEH(x,τ))"

AUX 37   "x is an event" $=$ df.
"for some time-interval τ, x is an event at time τ"
"EVNT(x)" $=$ df.
"($\exists$t)(τ_EVNT(x,τ))"

AUX 38   "person x expects, in time-interval τ, that event y will occur in time-interval τ'" $=$ df.
"x believes, in time-interval τ, that y is an event that occurs in time-interval τ', *and* τ is an earlier-and-discrete time-interval relative to τ'"
"XPC_EVNT(x,τ,y,τ')" $=$ df.
"BLF(τ_EVNT(y,τ'),x,τ) & EDT(τ,τ')"

AUX 39   "person x plans, in time-interval τ, that x exhibits **B**-behavior in time-interval τ'" $=$ df.
"x believes, in time-interval τ, that x exhibits **B**-behavior in time-interval τ', *and* τ is an earlier-and-discrete time-interval relative to τ'"
"PL_EXHIB_**B**_BEH(x,τ,**B**,τ')" $=$ df.
"BLF(**B**_BEH(**B**,x,τ'),x,τ) & EDT(τ,τ')"

AUX 40   "persons x and y mutually plan, in time-interval τ, that x will exhibit **B**-behavior in time-interval τ' *and* y will exhibit **B**'-behavior in time-interval τ''" $=$ df.
"person x plans, in time-interval τ, that x will exhibit **B**-behavior in time-interval τ', *and* person x expects, in time-interval τ, that person y will exhibit **B**'-behavior in time-interval τ'', *and* person y plans, in time-interval τ, that y will exhibit **B**'-behavior in

time-interval τ'', *and* person y expects, in time-interval τ, that
person x will exhibit **B**-behavior in time-interval τ'"
   "MUT_PL_SPECIF_BEH(x,**B**,y,**B**$'$,τ',τ'',τ)" = df.
   "PL_EXHIB_**B**_BEH(x,τ,**B**,τ') &
     XPC_EVNT(x,τ,**B**$'$_BEH(y,**B**$'$,τ'',τ)) &
     PL_EXHIB_**B**$'$_BEH(y,τ,**B**$'$,τ'') &
     XPC_EVNT(y,τ,**B**_BEH(x,**B**,τ',τ))"

Appendix E. Decision Terms:
Readings of Definientia

DEC 1 "**K** is an (**FG**)-for-**H**[b] functional predicate"

DEC 2 "x exhibits **K**(**FG**)-for-**H**[b] functional behavior in time-interval τ"

DEC 3 "**K** is a b-oriented functional predicate"

DEC 4 "x exhibits b-oriented functional **K**-behavior in time-interval τ"

DEC 5 "x exhibits b-oriented functional behavior"

DEC 6 "x exhibits functional behavior in time-interval τ"

DEC 7 "x exhibits overt purposive **K**(**FG**)-for-**H**[b] behavior in time-interval τ"

DEC 8 "x exhibits purposive **K**(**FG**)-for-**H**[b] behavior in time-interval τ"

DEC 9 "x exhibits purposive b-oriented behavior in time-interval τ"

DEC 10 "x exhibits purposive behavior in time-interval τ"

DEC 11 "x is a **K**(**FG**)-for-**H**[b] psychological individual in time-interval τ"

DEC 12 "x is a psychological individual in time-interval τ"

DEC 13   "x exhibits **K(FG)**-for-**H**[b] decision behavior in time-interval τ"

DEC 14   "x exhibits decision behavior in time-interval τ"

DEC 15   "x exhibits pseudo **K(FG)**-for-**H**[b] decision behavior in time-interval τ"

DEC 16   "x exhibits pseudo decision behavior in time-interval τ"

DEC 17   "x exhibits conscious **K(FG)**-for-**H**[b] decision behavior in time-interval τ"

DEC 18   "x exhibits conscious decision behavior in time-interval τ"

DEC 19   "x exhibits unconscious decision behavior in time-interval τ"

DEC 20   "x is an event that is **K(FG)**-for-**H**[b] cooperative for y in time-interval τ"

DEC 21   "x is an event that is cooperative for y in time-interval τ"

DEC 22   "x is an event that is **K(FG)**-for-**H**[b] conflicting with y in time-interval τ"

DEC 23   "x is an event that conflicts with y in time-interval τ"

DEC 24   "x is an event that is **K(FG)**-for-**H**[b] teleologically independent for y in time-interval τ"

DEC 25   "x is an event that is teleologically independent for y in time-interval τ"

DEC 26   "x is a group in time-interval τ"

DEC 27   "person x makes statement 'p' to person y in time-interval τ"

DEC 28   "person x agrees on 'p' with person y in time-interval τ"

DEC 29   "persons x and y mutually agree on 'p' in time-interval τ"

Appendix F. Decision Terms: Formal Definitions*

DEC 1 "**K** is an (**FG**)-for-**H**[b] functional predicate" = df.
"for all x, *if* x has **F**, *or if* x has **G**, *then* x has **K** *and* **F** is a
morphological predicate *and* **G** is a morphological predicate *and*
the y that is the fusion of **F** is disjunct from the z that is the fusion
of **G** *and* the fusion of **F** conduces that b will have **H** *and* the
fusion of **G** conduces that b will have **H**"
"SPC_FN_PRD(**K**{**F**, . . . ,**G**,**H**[b]})" = df.
"($\forall$x) ((**F**[x]^v**G**[x])$\supset$K[x]) & MRF(**F**) & MRF(**G**) &
((ιy)FU(**F**,y)ι(ιy)FU(**G**,y)) & **con**(FU(**F**,y),**H**[b]) &
con(FU(**G**,y),**H**[b])"

DEC 2 "x exhibits **K**(**FG**)-for-**H**[b] functional behavior in time-interval
τ" = df.
"**K** is an (**FG**)-for-**H**[b] functional predicate *and* the y that is the
interval-part of x in time-interval τ has **F** *or* the y that is the
interval-part of x in time-interval τ has **G** *and* **K** is a behavioral
predicate"
"SPC_FN_BEH(x,**K**{**F**, . . . ,**G**,**H**[b]} [x];τ)" = df.

---

* Beginning with DEC 1 and continuing through most of the following definitions,
the term "SPC" appears in the logical notation. This term signifies that the definition
refers to a specific predicate or predicates. A common locution to be found in these
definitions will be something like "**K**{**F**, . . . ,**G**,**H**[b]}." This refers to a particular
functional predicate, **K**, whose predicate components are the collection **F**, . . . ,**G**
and whose hoped-for, or expected, result is that individual *b* has **H**.

"SPC_FN_PRD($\mathbf{K}\{\mathbf{F}, \ldots, \mathbf{G}, \mathbf{H}[b]\}$) & ($\mathbf{F}[(\iota y)\mathrm{IP}(y,x,\tau)]$ ∨
$\mathbf{G}[(\iota y)\mathrm{IP}(y,x,\tau)])$"

DEC 3   "$\mathbf{K}$ is a b-oriented functional predicate" = df.
         "$\mathbf{K}$ is a functional predicate that is ($\mathbf{FG}$)-for-$\mathbf{H}[b]$, for some $\mathbf{F}$,
         $\mathbf{G}$, and $\mathbf{H}$"
              "FN_PRD_IND_ORNT($\mathbf{K}$,b)" = df.
              "SPC_FN_PRD($\mathbf{K}\{\ \underline{\mathbf{F}}, \ldots, \underline{\mathbf{G}}, \underline{\mathbf{H}}[b]\}$)"

DEC 4   "x exhibits b-oriented functional $\mathbf{K}$-behavior in time-interval τ"
         = df.
         "x exhibits functional $\mathbf{K}(\mathbf{FG})$-for-$\mathbf{H}[b]$ behavior in time-interval
         τ, for some $\mathbf{F}$, $\mathbf{G}$, and $\mathbf{H}$"
              "FN_$\mathbf{K}$_BEH_IND_b_ORNT(x,$\mathbf{K}[x]$,b,τ)" = df.
              "SPC_FN_BEH(x,$\mathbf{K}\{\underline{\mathbf{F}}, \ldots, \underline{\mathbf{G}},\underline{\mathbf{H}}$, [b]} [x]; τ)"

DEC 5   "x exhibits b-oriented functional behavior" = df.
         "x exhibits b-oriented functional $\mathbf{K}$-behavior in time-interval τ, for
         some $\mathbf{K}$"
              "FN_BEH_IND_b_ORNT(x, b, τ)" = df.
              "FN_$\mathbf{K}$_BEH_IND_b_ORNT(x, $\underline{\mathbf{K}}$ [x], b; τ)"

DEC 6   "x exhibits functional behavior in time-interval τ" = df.
         "for some y, x exhibits y-oriented functional behavior in time-
         interval τ"
              "FN_BEH(x, τ)" = df.
              "($\exists y$)(FN_BEH_IND_y_ORNT(x,y,τ))"

DEC 7   "x exhibits overt purposive $\mathbf{K}(\mathbf{FG})$-for-$\mathbf{H}[b]$ behavior in time-
         interval τ" = df.
         "for some y and y', both of which are discrete interval-parts of x
         in time-interval τ *and* both of which exhibit functional $\mathbf{K}(\mathbf{FG})$-
         for-$\mathbf{H}[b]$ behavior in time-interval τ, y has $\mathbf{F}$ and not $\mathbf{G}$ *and* y'
         has $\mathbf{G}$ and not $\mathbf{F}$"
              "SPC_O_PRP_BEH(y,$\mathbf{K}\{\mathbf{F}, \ldots, \mathbf{G}, \mathbf{H}[b]\}$ [y];τ)" = df.
              "($\exists y$)($\exists y'$)(DIP(y,y',x) & PART(y, τ) & PART(y', τ) &
              SPC_FN_BEH(y, $\mathbf{K}\{\mathbf{F}, \ldots, \mathbf{G}, \mathbf{H}[b]\}$ [y];τ) & $\mathbf{F}[y]$ &
              $-\mathbf{G}[y]$ & SPC_FN_BEH(y,'$\mathbf{K}\{\mathbf{F}, \ldots, \mathbf{G}, \mathbf{H}[b]\}$ [y']; τ) &
              $\mathbf{G}[y']$ & $-\mathbf{F}[y'])$"

DEC 8   "x exhibits purposive **K**(**FG**)-for-**H**[b] behavior in time-interval
τ" = df.
"x exhibits overt purposive **K**(**FG**)-for-**H**[b] behavior in time-
interval τ *or* there is a time-interval τ′ that is part of τ *and* x
satisfies an index of overt purposive **K**(**FG**)-for-**H**[b] behavior
in τ *and* (the y that is the interval-part of x in τ′ has **F** and does
not have **G** *or* the y that is the interval-part of x in τ′ has **G** and
does not have **F**)"
"SPC_PRP_BEH(x,**K**{**F**, . . . ,**G**,**H**[b]} [x];τ)" = df.
"SPC_O_PRP_BEH(x,**K**{**F**, . . . ,**G**,**H**[b]} [x];τ) ∨
    (∃τ′)(PART(τ′,τ) &
INDEX(SPC_O_PRP_BEH(x,**K**{**F**, . . . ,**G**,**H**[b]} [x];τ′)) &
(**F**[(ιy)IP(y,x,τ′)] & − **G**[(ιy)IP(y,x,τ′)] ∨
G[(ιy)IP(y,x,τ′)] & − **F**[(ιy)IP(y,x,τ′)])))"

DEC 9   "x exhibits purposive b-oriented behavior in time-interval τ" = df.
"x exhibits, for some **K**, **F**, **G**, and **H**, purposive **K**(**FG**)-for-
H[b] behavior in time-interval τ"
"PRP_BEH_IND_ORNT(x, b, τ)" = df.
"SPC_PRP_BEH(x, <u>**K**{**F**</u>, . . . ,<u>**G**,**H**</u>,[b]} [x];τ)"

DEC 10   "x exhibits purposive behavior in time-interval τ" = df.
"there is a y such that x exhibits purposive y-oriented behavior in
time-interval τ"
"PRP_BEH(x, τ)" = df.
"(∃y)(PRP_BEH_IND_y_ORNT(x, y, τ))"

DEC 11   "x is a **K**(**FG**)-for-**H**[b] psychological individual in time-
interval τ" = df.
"x exhibits purposive **K**(**FG**)-for-**H**[b] behavior in time-
interval τ *or* (x does not exhibit functional **K**(**FG**)-for-**H**[b]
behavior in time-interval τ *and* x satisfies an index of purposive
K(**FG**)-for-**H**[b] behavior in time-interval τ)"
"SPC_PSY_IND(x, **K**{**F**, . . . ,**G**,**H**[b]} [x];τ)" = df.
"SPC_PRP_BEH(x, **K**{**F**, . . . ,**G**,**H**[b]} [x];τ) ∨
− (SPC_FN_BEH(x, **K**{**F**, . . . ,**G**,**H**[b]} [x];τ)) &
INDEX(SPC_PRP_BEH(x, **K**{**F**, . . . ,**G**,**H**[b]} [x];τ))"

DEC 12   "x is a psychological individual in time-interval τ" = df.
"for some y and for some **K**, **F**, **G**, and **H**, x is a **K**(**FG**)-

for-**H**[y] psychological individual in time-interval τ"
"PSY_IND(x, τ)" = df.
"(∃y)SPC_PSY_IND(x, **K**{**F**, . . . ,**G**,**H**,[y]} [x];τ)"

DEC 13   "x exhibits **K**(**FG**)-for-**H**[b] decision behavior in time-interval
τ" = df.
"x exhibits purposive **K**(**FG**)-for-**H**[b] behavior in time-
interval τ"
"SPC_DEC_BEH(x, **K**{**F**, . . . ,**G**,**H**[b]} [x];τ)" = df.
"SPC_PRP_BEH(x, **K**{**F**, . . . ,**G**,**H**[b]} [x];τ)"

DEC 14   "x exhibits decision behavior in time-interval τ" = df.
"x exhibits purposive behavior in time-interval τ"
"DEC_BEH(x, τ)" = df.
"PRP_BEH(x, τ)"

DEC 15   "x exhibits pseudo **K**(**FG**)-for-**H**[b] decision behavior in time-
interval τ" = df.
"x exhibits behavior in time-interval τ *and* x has nonveridical
belief, in time-interval τ, that x exhibits **K**(**FG**)-for-**H**[b]
decision behavior in time-interval τ"
"PSD_SPC_DEC_BEH(x, **K**{**F**, . . . ,**G**,**H**[b]} [x];τ)" = df.
"BEH(x, τ) & NV_BLF(SPC_DEC_BEH((x, **K**{**F**, . . . ,
G,**H**[b]} [x];τ),x, τ))"

DEC 16   "x exhibits pseudo decision behavior in time-interval τ" = df.
"x exhibits behavior in time-interval τ *and* x has nonveridical
belief, in time-interval τ, that x exhibits decision behavior in
time-interval τ"
"PSD_DEC_BEH(x, τ)" = df.
"BEH(x, τ) & NV_BLF(DEC_BEH(x, τ),x, τ)"

DEC 17   "x exhibits conscious **K**(**FG**)-for-**H**[b] decision behavior in
time-interval τ" = df.
"x has veridical belief, in time-interval τ, that x exhibits
K(**FG**)-for-**H**[b] decision behavior in time-interval τ"
"CNS_SPC_DEC_BEH(x, **K**{**F**, . . . ,**G**,**H**[b]} [x];τ)" = df.
"V_BLF(SPC_DEC_BEH((x, **K**{**F**, . . . ,**G**,**H**[b]}
[x];τ),x, τ))"

DEC 18   "x exhibits conscious decision behavior in time-interval τ" $=$ df.
"x has veridical belief, in time-interval τ, that x exhibits decision behavior in time-interval τ"
   "CNS_DEC_BEH(x, τ)" $=$ df.
   "V_BLF(DEC_BEH(x, τ),x, τ)"

DEC 19   "x exhibits unconscious decision behavior in time-interval τ"
$=$ df.
"x exhibits decision behavior in time-interval τ *and* x does not believe, in time-interval τ, that x exhibits decision behavior in time-interval τ"
   "UCNS_DEC_BEH(x, τ)" $=$ df.
   "DEC_BEH(x, τ) & $-$(BLF(DEC_BEH(x, τ),x,τ)))"

DEC 20   "x is an event that is $\mathbf{K}(\mathbf{FG})$-for-$\mathbf{H}$[b] cooperative for y in time-interval τ" $=$ df.
"y is a $\mathbf{K}(\mathbf{FG})$-for-$\mathbf{H}$[b] psychological individual in time-interval τ *and* there are time-intervals τ' and τ'' such that τ' is an earlier-and-discrete time-interval relative to τ'' *and* x is an event *and* x is part of time-interval τ' *and* x conduces to: the z that is the interval-part of b in τ'' has $\mathbf{H}$"
   "SPC_CP_EVNT(x, y, $\mathbf{K}\{\mathbf{F}, \ldots, \mathbf{G}, \mathbf{H}$[b]$\}$ [y];τ)" $=$ df.
   "SPC_PSY_IND(y, $\mathbf{K}\{\mathbf{F}, \ldots, \mathbf{G}, \mathbf{H}$[b]$\}$ [y];τ) &
      $(\exists\tau')(\exists\tau'')$(INTVL($\tau'$) & INTVL($\tau''$) & EDT($\tau'$, τ'') &
      EVNT(x) & PART(x, τ') & **con**(x, $\mathbf{H}$[(ιz)IP(z, b, τ'')]))"

DEC 21   "x is an event that is cooperative for y in time-interval τ" $=$ df.
"for some z, and for some $\mathbf{K}, \mathbf{F}, \mathbf{G}$, and $\mathbf{H}$, x is an event that is $\mathbf{K}(\mathbf{FG})$-for-$\mathbf{H}$[z] cooperative for y in time-interval τ"
   "CP_EVNT(x,y,τ)" $=$ df.
   "$(\exists$z)(SPC_CP_EVNT(x, y, $\underline{\mathbf{K}}\{\underline{\mathbf{F}}, \ldots, \underline{\mathbf{G}},\underline{\mathbf{H}},$[z]$\}$ [y];τ))"

DEC 22   "x is an event that is $\mathbf{K}(\mathbf{FG})$-for-$\mathbf{H}$[b] conflicting with y in time-interval τ" $=$ df.
"y is a $\mathbf{K}(\mathbf{FG})$-for-$\mathbf{H}$[b] psychological individual in time-interval τ *and* there are time-intervals τ' and τ'' such that each is part of τ *and* τ' is earlier than and discrete from τ'' *and* x is an event *and* x conduces to: the z that is the interval-part of b in τ'' does not have $\mathbf{H}$"

"SPC_CF_EVNT(x, y, **K**{**F**, . . . ,**G**,**H**[b]} [y];τ)" = df.
"SPC_PSY_IND(y, **K**{**F**, . . . ,**G**,**H**[b]} [y];τ) &
(∃τ′)(∃τ″)(INTVL(τ′) & INTVL(τ″) & PART(τ′,τ) &
PART(τ″,τ) & EDT(τ′,τ″) & EVNT(x) &
con(x, − **H**(ιz)IP(z, b, τ″)])"

DEC 23   "x is an event that conflicts with y in time-interval τ" = df.
"for some z and for some **K**, **F**, **G**, and **H**, x is an event that is
K(**FG**)-for-**H**[z] conflicting with y in time-interval τ"
"CF_EVNT(x, y, τ)" = df.
"(∃z) (SPC_CF_EVNT(x, y, <u>**K**{**F**</u>, . . . ,<u>**G**,**H**</u>,[z]} [y];τ))"

DEC 24   "x is an event that is **K**(**FG**)-for-**H**[b] teleologically
independent for y in time-interval τ" = df.
"x is an event that is not **K**(**FG**)-for-**H**[b] cooperative for y in
time-interval τ *and* x is an event that is not **K**(**FG**)-for-**H**[b]
conflicting for y in time-interval τ"
"SPC_TL_EVNT(x, y, **K**{**F**, . . . ,**G**,**H**[b]} [y];τ)" = df.
"− SPC_CP_EVNT(x, y, **K**{**F**, . . . ,**G**,**H**[b]} [y];τ) &
− (SPC_CF_EVNT(x, y, **K**{**F**, . . . ,**G**,**H**[b]} [y];τ))"

DEC 25   "x is an event that is teleologically independent for y in time-
interval τ" = df.
"x is an event that is not cooperative for y in time-interval τ *and* x
is an event that is not conflicting for y in time-interval τ"
"TL_EVNT(x, y, τ)" = df.
"− (CP_EVNT(x, y, τ)) & − (CF_EVNT(x, y, τ))"

DEC 26   "x is a group in time-interval τ" = df.
"(there is a w and there is a w′ such that both w and w′ are
psychological individuals in time-interval τ *and* w is part of x *and*
w′ is part of x) *and* (for all y, y is a psychological individual in
time-interval τ *and* (for all w and for all w′, (*if* w is part of y *and*
w′ is part of y *and* both w and w′ are psychological individuals
in time-interval τ, *then* w overlaps w′)) *and* (there is a z such that
if z is part of y *and* z is part of x, *then* y is part of x)) *and* (for all
z, *if* z overlaps x, *then* (there is a u such that u is a psychological
individual in time-interval τ *and* z overlaps u))"
"GP(x, τ)" = df.
"(∃w) (∃w′) (PSY_IND(w, τ) & PSY_IND(w′, τ) &
PART(w,x) & PART(w′,x)) & (∀y) (PSY_IND(y, τ) &

$(\forall w)(\forall w')(PART(w,y)$ & $PART(w',y)$ & $PSY\_IND(w, \tau)$ &
$PSY\_IND(w', \tau) \supset$ **overlaps**$(w,w'))$ & $(\exists z)(PART(z,y)$ &
$PART(z,x) \supset PART(y,x))))$ & $(\forall z)$ (**overlaps**$(z,x) \supset$
$(\exists u)$ $(PSY\_IND(u, \tau)$ & **overlaps**$(z, u)))$"

DEC 27   "person x makes statement 'p' to person y in time-interval τ"
          $=$ df.
          "person x exhibits purposive **K**(**FG**)-for-(y believes, in time-
          interval τ, that p) behavior in time-interval τ"
          "STATES(x,p,y,τ)" $=$ df.
          "SPECIF_PRP_BEH $(x,$ **K**$\{$**F**$, \ldots,$**G**$,$ BLF$(p,y,\tau)[x],$ $\tau)$"

DEC 28   "person x agrees on 'p' with person y in time-interval τ" $=$ df.
          "person y makes statement 'p' to person x in time-interval τ *and*
          person x believes in time-interval τ that p"
          "AGR(x,p,y,τ)" $=$ df.
          "STATES(x,p,y,τ) & BLF(p,x,τ)"

DEC 29   "persons x and y mutually agree on 'p' in time-interval τ" $=$ df.
          "person x agrees on 'p' with person y in time-interval τ *and*
          person y agrees on 'p' with person x in time-interval τ"
          "MUT_AGR(x,y,p,τ)" $=$ df.
          "AGR(x,p,y,τ) & AGR(y,p,x,τ)"

Appendix G. Socioeconomic Terms: Readings of Definientia

SOC 1   "x is a person who cooperates **L(MN)**-for-**J**[b] with person y **K(FG)**-for-**H**[a] in time-interval τ"

SOC 2   "x is a person who cooperates **L(MN)**-for-**H**[a] convergently with person y **K(FG)**-for-**H**[a] in time-interval τ"

SOC 3   "x is a person who cooperates **K(FG)**-for-**J**[b] divergently with person y **K(FG)**-for-**H**[a] in time-interval τ"

SOC 4   "x is a person who cooperates **K(FG)**-for-**H**[a] in concert with person y in time-interval τ"

SOC 5   "x is a person who accommodatingly cooperates with person y **K(FG)**-for-**H**[a] in time-interval τ"

SOC 6   "x is a person who cooperates with person y in time-interval τ"

SOC 7   "x is a person who conflicts **L(MN)**-for-**J**[b] with person y **K(FG)**-for-**H**[a] in time-interval τ"

SOC 8   "x is a person who conflicts **L(MN)**-for-**H**[a] convergently with person y **K(FG)**-for-**H**[a] in time-interval τ"

SOC 9   "x is a person who conflicts **K(FG)**-for-**J**[b] divergently with person y **K(FG)**-for-**H**[a] in time-interval τ"

SOC 10   "x is a person who conflicts **K(FG)**-for-**H**[a] in parallel with person y in time-interval τ"

SOC 11   "x is a person who is in head-on conflict with person y **K**(**FG**)-for-**H**[a] in time-interval τ"

SOC 12   "x is a person who conflicts with person y **K**(**FG**)-for-**H**[a] in time-interval τ"

SOC 13   "x is a person who conflicts with person y in time-interval τ"

SOC 14   "x is a person who is teleologically independent **L**(**MN**)-for-**J**[b] for person y **K**(**FG**)-for-**H**[a] in time-interval τ"

SOC 15   "x is a person who is teleologically independent **L**(**MN**)-for-**H**[a] convergently for person y **K**(**FG**)-for-**H**[a] in time-interval τ"

SOC 16   "x is a person who is teleologically independent **K**(**FG**)-for-**J**[b] divergently for person y **K**(**FG**)-for-**H**[a] in time-interval τ"

SOC 17   "x is a person who is teleologically independent **K**(**FG**)-for-**H**[a] in concert with person y in time-interval τ"

SOC 18   "x is a person who is teleologically independent with person y **K**(**FG**)-for-**H**[a] in time-interval τ"

SOC 19   "x is a person who is teleologically independent with person y in time-interval τ"

SOC 20   "x is a person who deliberately cooperates **L**(**MN**)-for-**J**[b] with person y **K**(**FG**)-for-**H**[a] in time-interval τ"

SOC 21   "x is a person who deliberately cooperates **L**(**MN**)-for-**H**[a] convergently with person y **K**(**FG**)-for-**H**[a] in time-interval τ"

SOC 22   "x is a person who deliberately cooperates **K**(**FG**)-for-**J**[b] divergently with person y **K**(**FG**)-for-**H**[a] in time-interval τ"

SOC 23   "x is a person who deliberately cooperates **K**(**FG**)-for-**H**[a] in concert with person y in time-interval τ"

SOC 24   "x is a person who deliberately cooperates with person y in time-interval τ"

SOC 25   "x is a person who deliberately conflicts **L**(**MN**)-for-**J**[b] with person y **K**(**FG**)-for-**H**[a] in time-interval τ"

SOC 26   "x is a person who deliberately conflicts **L(MN)**-for-**H**[a] convergently with person y **K(FG)**-for-**H**[a] in time-interval τ"

SOC 27   "x is a person who deliberately conflicts **K(FG)**-for-**J**[b] divergently with person y **K(FG)**-for-**H**[a] in time-interval τ"

SOC 28   "x is a person who is deliberately in head-on conflict **K(FG)**-for-not-**H**[a] with person y **K(FG)**-for-**H**[a] in time-interval τ"

SOC 29   "x is a person who deliberately conflicts with person y in time-interval τ"

SOC 30   "x is a person who is deliberately teleologically independent **L(MN)**-for-**J**[b] for person y **K(FG)**-for-**H**[a] in time-interval τ"

SOC 31   "x is a person who is deliberately teleologically independent **L(MN)**-for-**H**[a] convergently for person y **K(FG)**-for-**H**[a] in time-interval τ"

SOC 32   "x is a person who is deliberately teleologically independent **K(FG)**-for-**J**[b] divergently for person y **K(FG)**-for-**H**[a] in time-interval τ"

SOC 33   "x is a person who is deliberately teleologically independent **K(FG)**-for-**H**[a] in concert for person y in time-interval τ"

SOC 34   "x and y symmetrically mutually cooperate **L(MN)**-for-**J**[b], **K(FG)**-for-**H**[a], in time-interval τ"

SOC 35   "x and y symmetrically mutually cooperate **L(MN)**-for-**H**[a], **K(FG)**-for-**H**[a], convergently in time-interval τ"

SOC 36   "x and y symmetrically mutually cooperate **K(FG)**-for-**J**[b], **K(FG)**-for-**H**[a], divergently in time-interval τ"

SOC 37   "x and y symmetrically mutually cooperate **K(FG)**-for-**H**[a] in concert in time-interval τ"

SOC 38   "x and y symmetrically mutually conflict **L(MN)**-for-**J**[b], **K(FG)**-for-**H**[a], in time-interval τ"

SOC 39   "x and y symmetrically mutually conflict **L(MN)**-for-**H**[a], **K(FG)**-for-**H**[a], convergently in time-interval τ"

SOC 40 "x and y symmetrically mutually conflict **K(FG)**-for-**J**[b], **K(FG)**-for-**H**[a], divergently in time-interval τ"

SOC 41 "x and y are in symmetric mutual competition **K(FG)**-for-**H**[a] in time-interval τ"

SOC 42 "x and y symmetrically mutually conflict **K(FG)**-for-**H**[a], **K(FG)**-for-not-**H**[a], head-on in time-interval τ"

SOC 43 "x and y are symmetrically mutually teleologically independent **L(MN)**-for-**J**[b], **K(FG)**-for-**H**[a], in time-interval τ"

SOC 44 "x and y are symmetrically mutually teleologically independent **L(MN)**-for-**H**[a], **K(FG)**-for-**H**[a], convergently in time-interval τ"

SOC 45 "x and y are symmetrically mutually teleologically independent **K(FG)**-for-**J**[b], **K(FG)**-for-**H**[a], divergently in time-interval τ"

SOC 46 "x and y are symmetrically mutually teleologically independent **K(FG)**-for-**H**[a], **K(FG)**-for-**H**[a], in concert in time-interval τ"

SOC 47 "x **L(MN)**-for-**J**[b] *and* **K(FG)**-for-**H**[a], *and* y **O(PQ)**-for-**I**[c] *and* **R(ST)**-for-**U**[d], are persons who are quasi-symmetrically mutually cooperating in time-interval τ"

SOC 48 "x **L(MN)**-for-**J**[b] *and* **L(MN)**-for-**H**[a], *and* y **O(PQ)**-for-**I**[c] *and* **O(PQ)**-for-**F**[d], are persons who are quasi-symmetrically mutually conflicting divergently in time-interval τ"

SOC 49 "x and y are asymmetrically mutually interacting persons, x cooperating **L(MN)**-for-**J**[b] with y **K(FG)**-for-**J**[b] convergently, y conflicting **R(ST)**-for-not-**F**[d] with x **R(ST)**-for-**F**[d] head-on in time-interval τ"

SOC 50 "x and y are **K(FG)**-for-**H**[a] rivals in time-interval τ"

SOC 51 "person x takes revenge on person y in time-interval τ'"

SOC 52 "person x avenges person z on person y in time-interval τ"

SOC 53 "person x makes a certain **K(FG)**-for-**H**[a] investment in time-interval τ with person y **L(MN)**-for-**J**[b] in time-interval τ'"

SOC 54   "persons x and y enter into a **K**(**FG**)-for-**H**[a]-time-τ', **L**(**MN**)-for-**J**[b]-time-τ'', agreement, in time-interval τ"

SOC 55   "person x pays **K**(**FG**)-for-**H**[y] to person y in time-interval τ"

SOC 56   "person x trades **H** in time-interval τ to person y for **J** in time-interval τ'"

SOC 57   "persons x and y enter into a **K**(**FG**)-for-**H**[a]-time-τ', **L**(**MN**)-for-**J**[b]-time-τ'', contract, in time-interval τ, with penalties **R**(**ST**)-for-**U**[c], **O**(**PQ**)-for-**V**[d]"

Appendix H. Socioeconomic Terms:
Formal Definitions

SOC 1 "x is a person who cooperates $\mathbf{L(MN)}$-for-$\mathbf{J}$[b] with person y $\mathbf{K(FG)}$-for-$\mathbf{H}$[a] in time-interval τ" = df.

"x exhibits overt purposive $\mathbf{L(MN)}$-for-$\mathbf{J}$[b] behavior in time-interval τ *and* there is a z that is the interval-part of x in time-interval τ *and* z is an event that is $\mathbf{K(FG)}$-for-$\mathbf{H}$[a] cooperative with y in time-interval τ"

"SPC_CP_PRS(x,$\mathbf{L}\{\mathbf{M}$, . . . , $\mathbf{N},\mathbf{J}$[b]} [x]; y, $\mathbf{K}\{\mathbf{F}$, . . . , $\mathbf{G},\mathbf{H}$[a]}[y];τ)" = df.

"SPC_O_PRP_BEH(x,$\mathbf{L}\{\mathbf{M}$, . . . ,$\mathbf{N},\mathbf{J}$[b]} [x];τ) & ($\exists$z)(IP(z,x,t) & SPC_CP_EVNT(z,y,$\mathbf{K}\{\mathbf{F}$, . . . ,$\mathbf{G},\mathbf{H}$[a]} [y];τ)"

SOC 2 "x is a person who cooperates $\mathbf{L(MN)}$-for-$\mathbf{H}$[a] convergently with person y $\mathbf{K(FG)}$-for-$\mathbf{H}$[a] in time-interval τ" = df.

"x is a person who cooperates $\mathbf{L(MN)}$-for-$\mathbf{H}$[a] with person y $\mathbf{K(FG)}$-for-$\mathbf{H}$[a] in time-interval τ"

"CNV_SPC_CP_PRS(x,$\mathbf{L}\{\mathbf{M}$, . . . ,$\mathbf{N},\mathbf{H}$[a]} [x];y,$\mathbf{K}\{\mathbf{F}$, . . . , $\mathbf{G},\mathbf{H}$[a]}[y];τ)" = df.

"SPC_CP_PRS(x,$\mathbf{L}\{\mathbf{M}$, . . . ,$\mathbf{N},\mathbf{H}$[a]} [x]; y,$\mathbf{K}\{\mathbf{F}$, . . . , $\mathbf{G},\mathbf{H}$[a]} [y];τ)"

SOC 3 "x is a person who cooperates $\mathbf{K(FG)}$-for-$\mathbf{J}$[b] divergently with person y $\mathbf{K(FG)}$-for-$\mathbf{H}$[a] in time-interval τ" = df.

"x is a person who cooperates $\mathbf{K(FG)}$-for-$\mathbf{J}$[b] with person y $\mathbf{K(FG)}$-for-$\mathbf{H}$[a] in time-interval τ"

"DIV_SPC_CP_PRS(x,**K**{**F**, . . . ,**G**,**J**[b]} [x];y,**K**{**F**,
. . . , **G**,**H**[a]} [y];τ)" = df.
"SPC_CP_PRS(x,**K**{**F**, . . . ,**G**,**J**[b]} [x];y,**K**{**F**, . . . ,
G,**H**[a]} [y];τ)"

SOC 4   "x is a person who cooperates **K**(**FG**)-for-**H**[a] in concert with
person y in time-interval τ" = df.
"x is a person who cooperates **K**(**FG**)-for-**H**[a] with person y
K(**FG**)-for-**H**[a] in time-interval τ"
    "SPC_CP_PRS_CCR(x,y,**K**{**F**, . . . ,**G**,**H**[a]} [y];τ)" = df.
    "SPC_CP_PRS(x,**K**{**F**, . . . ,**G**,**H**[a]} [x];y,**K**{**F**, . . . ,
    G,**H**[a]} [y];τ)"

SOC 5   "x is a person who accommodatingly cooperates with person y
K(**FG**)-for-**H**[a] in time-interval τ" = df.
"for some predicates **L**, **M**, **N**, and **J** *and* some person z, x is a
person who cooperates **L**(**MN**)-for-**J**[z] with person y
K(**FG**)-for-**H**[a] in time-interval τ"
    "ACC_CP_PRS_WITH_PRS(x,y,**K**{**F**, . . . ,**G**,**H**[a]} [y];τ)"
    = df.
    "(∃z)SPC_CP_PRS(x,**L**{**M**, . . . ,**N**,**J**[z]} ;y,**K**{**F**, . . . ,
    G,**H**[a]} [y];τ)"

SOC 6   "x is a person who cooperates with person y in time-interval τ"
= df.
"for some predicates **K**, **F**, **G**, and **H** *and* some person w, x is
a person who accommodatingly cooperates with person y
K(**FG**)-for-**H**[w] in time-interval τ"
    "CP_PRS_WITH_PRS(x,y,τ)" = df.
    "(∃z)(∃w)ACC_CP_PRS(x,**L**{**M**, . . . ,**N**,**J**[z]} [x];y,**K**{**F**,
    . . . ,**G**,**H**[w]} [y];τ)"

SOC 7   "x is a person who conflicts **L**(**MN**)-for-**J**[b] with person y
K(**FG**)-for-**H**[a] in time-interval τ" = df.
"x exhibits overt purposive **L**(**MN**)-for-**J**[b] behavior in time-
interval τ *and* there is a z that is the interval-part of x in time-
interval τ *and* z is an event that is **K**(**FG**)-for-**H**[a] conflicting
with y in time-interval τ"
    "SPC_CF_PRS(x,**L**{**M**, . . . ,**N**,**J**[b]} [x];y,**K**{**F**, . . . ,
    G,**H**[a]} [y];τ)" = df.
    "SPC_O_PRP_BEH(x,**L**{**M**, . . . ,**N**,**J**[b]} [x];τ) &

(∃z)IP(z,x,τ) & SPC_CF_EVNT(z,y,**K**{**F**, . . . ,**G**,**H**[a]}
[y];τ)"

SOC 8   "x is a person who conflicts **L**(**MN**)-for-**H**[a] convergently
with person y **K**(**FG**)-for-**H**[a] in time-interval τ" = df.
"x is a person who conflicts **L**(**MN**)-for-**H**[a] with person y
K(**FG**)-for-**H**[a] in time-interval τ"
"CNV_SPC_CF_PRS(x,**L**{**M**, . . . ,**N**,**H**[a]} [x];y,**K**{**F**,
. . . ,**G**,**H**[a]} [y];τ)" = df.
"SPC_CF_PRS(x,**L**{**M**, . . . ,**N**,**H**[a]} [x];y,**K**{**F**, . . . ,
G,**H**[a]} [y];τ)"

SOC 9   "x is a person who conflicts **K**(**FG**)-for-**J**[b] divergently with
person y **K**(**FG**)-for-**H**[a] in time-interval τ" = df.
"x is a person who conflicts **K**(**FG**)-for-**J**[b] with person y
K(**FG**)-for-**H**[a] in time-interval τ"
"DIV_SPC_CF_PRS(x,**K**{**F**, . . . ,**G**,**J**[b]} [x];y,**K**{**F**,
. . . , **G**,**H**[a]} [y];τ)" = df.
"SPC_CF_PRS(x,**K**{**F**, . . . ,**G**,**J**[b]} [x];y,**K**{**F**, . . . ,
G,**H**[a]} [y];τ)"

SOC 10 "x is a person who conflicts **K**(**FG**)-for-**H**[a] in parallel with
person y in time-interval τ" = df.
"x is a person who conflicts **K**(**FG**)-for-**H**[a] with person y
K(**FG**)-for-**H**[a] in time-interval τ"
"PRL_SPC_CF_PRS(x,**K**{**F**, . . . ,**G**,**H**[a]} [x];y,**K**{**F**,
. . . , **G**,**H**[a]} [y];τ)" = df.
"SPC_CF_PRS(x,**K**{**F**, . . . ,**G**,**H**[a]} [x];y,**K**{**F**, . . . ,
G,**H**[a]} [y];τ)"

SOC 11 "x is a person who is in head-on conflict with person y **K**(**FG**)-
for-**H**[a] in time-interval τ" = df.
"x is a person who conflicts **K**(**FG**)-for-not-**H**[a] with person y
K(**FG**)-for-**H**[a] in time-interval τ"
"H_ON_SPC_CF_PRS(x,**K**{**F**, . . . ,**G**, − **H**[a]} [x];y,**K**{**F**,
. . . ,**G**,**H**[a]} [y];τ)" = df.
"SPC_CF_PRS(x,**K**{**F**, . . . ,**G**, − **H**[a]} [x];y,**K**{**F**, . . . ,
G,**H**[a]} [y];τ)"

SOC 12 "x is a person who conflicts with person y **K**(**FG**)-for-**H**[a] in
time-interval τ" = df.

"for some predicates **L**, **M**, **N**, and **J** *and* some person z, x is a person who conflicts **L**(**MN**)-for-**J**[z] with person y **K**(**FG**)-for-**H**[a] in time-interval τ"

"CF_PRS(x;y,**K**{**F**, . . . ,**G**,**H**[a]} [y];τ)" = df.

"(∃z)SPC_CF_PRS(x,**L**{<u>**M**</u>, . . . ,<u>**N**</u>,**J**[z]} [x];y,**K**{**F**, . . . , **G**,**H**[a]} [y];τ)"

SOC 13 "x is a person who conflicts with person y in time-interval τ" = df.

"for some predicates **K**, **F**, **G**, and **H** *and* some person w, x is a person who conflicts with person y **K**(**FG**)-for-**H**[w] in time-interval τ"

"CF_PRS_WITH_PRS(x,y,τ)" = df.

"(∃z)(∃w)CF_PRS(x,**L**{<u>**M**</u>, . . . ,<u>**N**</u>,**J**[z]} [x];y,<u>**K**</u>{**F**, . . . ,<u>**G**</u>,<u>**H**</u>[w]} [y];τ)"

SOC 14 "x is a person who is teleologically independent **L**(**MN**)-for-**J**[b] for person y **K**(**FG**)-for-**H**[a] in time-interval τ" = df.

"x exhibits overt purposive **L**(**MN**)-for-**J**[b] behavior in time-interval τ *and* there is a z that is the interval-part of x in time-interval τ *and* z is an event that is **K**(**FG**)-for-**H**[a] teleologically independent for y in time-interval τ"

"SPC_TL_PRS(x,**L**{**M**, . . . ,**N**,**J**[b]} [x];y,**K**{**F**, . . . , **G**,**H**[a]} [y];τ)" = df.

"SPC_O_PRP_BEH(x,**L**{**M**, . . . ,**N**,**J**[b]} [x];τ) & (∃z)IP(z,y,τ) & SPC_TL_EVNT(z,y,**K**{**F**, . . . ,**G**,**H**[b]} [y];τ)"

SOC 15 "x is a person who is teleologically independent **L**(**MN**)-for-**H**[a] convergently for person y **K**(**FG**)-for-**H**[a] in time-interval τ" = df.

"x is a person who is teleologically independent **L**(**MN**)-for-**H**[a] for person y **K**(**FG**)-for-**H**[a] in time-interval τ"

"CNV_SPC_TL_PRS(x,**L**{**M**, . . . ,**N**,**H**[a]} [x];y,**K**{**F**, . . . ,**G**,**H**[a]} [y];τ)" = df.

"SPC_TL_PRS(x,**L**{**M**, . . . ,**N**,**H**[a]} [x];y,**K**{**F**, . . . , **G**,**H**[a]} [y];τ)"

SOC 16 "x is a person who is teleologically independent **K**(**FG**)-for-**J**[b] divergently for person y **K**(**FG**)-for-**H**[a] in time-interval τ" = df.

"x is a person who is teleologically independent **K**(**FG**)-for-**J**[b] for person y **K**(**FG**)-for-**H**[a] in time-interval τ"
   "DIV_SPC_TL_PRS(x,**K**{**F**, . . . ,**G**,**J**[b]} [x];y,**K**{**F**, . . . , **G**,**H**[a]} [y];τ)" = df.
   "SPC_TL_PRS(x,**K**{**F**, . . . ,**G**,**J**[b]} [x];y,**K**{**F**, . . . , **G**,**H**[a]} [y];τ)"

SOC 17   "x is a person who is teleologically independent **K**(**FG**)-for-**H**[a] in concert with person y in time-interval τ" = df.
   "x is a person who is teleologically independent **K**(**FG**)-for-**H**[a] for person y **K**(**FG**)-for-**H**[a] in time-interval τ"
   "SPC_TL_PRS_CCR(x,**K**{**F**, . . . ,**G**,**H**[a]} [x];y,**K**{**F**, . . . , **G**,**H**[a]} [y];τ)" = df.
   "SPC_TL_PRS(x,**K**{**F**, . . . ,**G**,**H**[a]} [x];y,**K**{**F**, . . . , **G**,**H**[a]} [y];τ)"

SOC 18   "x is a person who is teleologically independent with person y **K**(**FG**)-for-**H**[a] in time-interval τ" = df.
   "for some predicates **L**, **M**, **N**, and **J**, person x is teleologically independent **L**(**MN**)-for-**J**[b] for person y in time-interval τ"
   "EXST_PREDS_TL_PRS(x,y,**K**{**F**, . . . ,**G**,**H**[a]} [y];τ)" = df.
   "SPC_TL_PRS(x,<u>**L**</u>{<u>**M**</u>, . . . ,<u>**N**</u>,**J**[b]} [x];y,**K**{**F**, . . . , **G**,**H**[a]} [y];τ)"

SOC 19   "x is a person who is teleologically independent with person y in time-interval τ" = df.
   "for some predicates **K**, **F**, **G**, and **H** *and* some person w, x is a person who is teleologically independent with person y **K**(**FG**)-for-**H**[a] in time-interval τ"
   "EXST_PREDS_AND_OBJ_TL_PRS(x,y;τ)" = df.
   "(∃w)EXST_PREDS_TL_PRS(x,y,**K**{**F**, . . . ,**G**,**H**[w]} [y];τ)"

SOC 20   "x is a person who deliberately cooperates **L**(**MN**)-for-**J**[b] with person y **K**(**FG**)-for-**H**[a] in time-interval τ" = df.
   "x is a person who cooperates **L**(**MN**)-for-**J**[b] with person y **K**(**FG**)-for-**H**[a] in time-interval τ *and* x veridically believes that x is a person who cooperates **L**(**MN**)-for-**J**[b] with person y **K**(**FG**)-for-**H**[a] in time-interval τ"

"DLB_SPC_CP_PRS(x,**L**{**M**, . . . ,**N**,**J**[b]} [x];y,**K**{**F**,
. . . , **G**,**H**[a]} [y];τ)" = df.
"SPC_CP_PRS(x,**L**{**M**, . . . ,**N**,**J**[b]} [x];y,**K**{**F**, . . . ,
G,**H**[a]} [y];τ) & V_BLF_(SPC_CP_PRS(x,**L**{**M**, . . . ,
N,**J**[b]} [x];y,**K**{**F**, . . . ,**G**,**H**[a]} [y];τ),x,τ)"

SOC 21   "x is a person who deliberately cooperates **L**(**MN**)-for-**H**[a]
convergently with person y **K**(**FG**)-for-**H**[a] in time-interval τ"
= df.
"x is a person who deliberately cooperates **L**(**MN**)-for-**H**[a]
with person y **K**(**FG**)-for-**H**[a] in time-interval τ"
"CNV_DLB_SPC_CP_PRS(x,**L**{**M**, . . . ,**N**,**H**[a]}
[x];y,**K**{**F**, . . . ,**G**,**H**[a]} [y];τ)" = df.
"DLB_SPC_CP_PRS(x,**L**{**M**, . . . ,**N**,**H**[a]} [x];y,**K**{**F**,
. . . ,**G**,**H**[a]} [y];τ)"

SOC 22   "x is a person who deliberately cooperates **K**(**FG**)-for-**J**[b]
divergently with person y **K**(**FG**)-for-**H**[a] in time-interval τ"
= df.
"x is a person who deliberately cooperates **K**(**FG**)-for-**J**[b]
with person y **K**(**FG**)-for-**H**[a] in time-interval τ"
"DIV_DLB_SPC_CP_PRS(x,**K**{**F**, . . . ,**G**,**J**[b]}
[x];y,**K**{**F**, . . . ,**G**,**H**[a]} [y];τ)" = df.
"DLB_SPC_CP_PRS(x,**K**{**F**, . . . , **G**,**J**[b]} [x];y,**K**{**F**,
. . . , **G**,**H**[a]} [y];τ)"

SOC 23   "x is a person who deliberately cooperates **K**(**FG**)-for-**H**[a] in
concert with person y in time-interval τ" = df.
"x is a person who deliberately cooperates **K**(**FG**)-for-**H**[a]
with person y **K**(**FG**)-for-**H**[a] in time-interval τ"
"DLB_SPC_CP_CCR_PRS(x,**K**{**F**, . . . ,**G**,**H**[a]}
[x];y,**K**{**F**, . . . , **G**,**H**[a]} [y];τ)" = df.
"DLB_SPC_CP_PRS(x,**K**{**F**, . . . ,**G**,**H**[a]} [x];y,**K**{**F**,
. . . , **G**,**H**[a]} [y];τ)"

SOC 24   "x is a person who deliberately cooperates with person y in time-
interval τ" = df.
"for some predicates **K**, **F**, **G**, **H**, **L**, **M**, **N**, and **J** *and* for
some persons w and z, x is a person who deliberately cooperates
L(**MN**)-for-**J**[b] with person y **K**(**FG**)-for-**H**[a] in time-
interval τ"

"DLB_CP_PRS(x,y,τ)" = df.
"(∃w)(∃z)DLB_SPC_CP_PRS(w,**L**{**M**, . . . ,**N**,**J**[b]}
[w];z,**K**{**F**, . . . ,**G**,**H**[a]} [z];τ)"

SOC 25   "x is a person who deliberately conflicts **L**(**MN**)-for-**J**[b] with
person y **K**(**FG**)-for-**H**[a] in time-interval τ" = df.
"x is a person who conflicts **L**(**MN**)-for-**J**[b] with person y
K(**FG**)-for-**H**[a] in time-interval τ *and* x veridically believes
that x is a person who conflicts **L**(**MN**)-for-**J**[b] with person y
K(**FG**)-for-**H**[a] in time-interval τ"
   "DLB_SPC_CF_PRS(x,**L**{**M**, . . . ,**N**,**J**[b]} [x];y,**K**{**F**,
   . . . , **G**,**H**[a]} [y];τ)" = df.
   "SPC_CF_PRS(x,**L**{**M**, . . . ,**N**,**J**[b]} [x];y,**K**{**F**, . . . ,
   G,**H**[a]} [y];τ) & V_BLF(SPC_CF_PRS(x,**L**{**M**, . . . ,
   N,**J**[b]} [x];y,**K**{**F**, . . . ,**G**,**H**[a]} [y];τ), x,τ)"

SOC 26   "x is a person who deliberately conflicts **L**(**MN**)-for-**H**[a]
convergently with person y **K**(**FG**)-for-**H**[a] in time-interval τ"
= df.
"x is a person who deliberately conflicts **L**(**MN**)-for-**H**[a] with
person y **K**(**FG**)-for-**H**[a] in time-interval τ"
   "CNV_DLB_SPC_CF_PRS(x,**L**{**M**, . . . ,**N**,**H**[a]}
   [x];y,**K**{**F**, . . . ,**G**,**H**[a]} [y];τ)" = df.
   "DLB_SPC_CF_PRS(x,**L**{**M**, . . . ,**N**,**H**[a]} [x];y,**K**{**F**,
   . . . ,**G**,**H**[a]} [y];τ)"

SOC 27   "x is a person who deliberately conflicts **K**(**FG**)-for-**J**[b]
divergently with person y **K**(**FG**)-for-**H**[a] in time-interval τ"
= df.
"x is a person who deliberately conflicts **K**(**FG**)-for-**J**[b] with
person y **K**(**FG**)-for-**H**[a] in time-interval τ"
   "DIV_DLB_SPC_CF_PRS(x,**K**{**F**, . . . ,**G**,**J**[b]}
   [x];y,**K**{**F**, . . . ,**G**,**H**[a]} [y];τ)" = df.
   "DLB_SPC_CF_PRS(x,**K**{**F**, . . . ,**G**,**J**[b]} [x];y,**K**{**F**,
   . . . , **G**,**H**[a]} [y];τ)"

SOC 28   "x is a person who is deliberately in head-on conflict **K**(**FG**)-
for-not-**H**[a] with person y **K**(**FG**)-for-**H**[a] in time-interval τ"
= df.
"x is a person who deliberately conflicts **K**(**FG**)-for-not-**H**[a]
with person y **K**(**FG**)-for-**H**[a] in time-interval τ"

"DLB_H_ON_SPC_CF_PRS(x,**K**{**F**, . . . ,**G**, − **H**[a]}
[x];y,**K**{**F**, . . . ,**G**,**H**[a]} [y];τ)" = df.
"DLB_SPC_CF_PRS(x,**K**{**F**, . . . ,**G**, − **H**[a]} [x];y,**K**{**F**,
. . . ,**G**,**H**[a]} [y];τ)"

SOC 29   "x is a person who deliberately conflicts with person y in time-
interval τ" = df.
"for some predicates **K**, **F**, **G**, **H**, **L**, **M**, **N**, and **J** *and* for
some persons w and z, x is a person who deliberately conflicts
L(**MN**)-for-**J**[b] with person y **K**(**FG**)-for-**H**[a] in time-
interval τ"
  "DLB_CF_PRS(x,y,τ)" = df.
  "(∃w)(∃z)DLB_SPC_CF_PRS(w,**L**{**M**, . . . ,**N**,**J**[b]}
  [w];z,**K**{**F**, . . . ,**G**,**H**[a]} [z];τ)"

SOC 30   "x is a person who is deliberately teleologically independent
L(**MN**)-for-**J**[b] for person y **K**(**FG**)-for-**H**[a] in time-
interval τ" = df.
"x is a person who is teleologically independent **L**(**MN**)-for-
J[b] for person y **K**(**FG**)-for-**H**[a] in time-interval τ *and* x
veridically believes that x is a person who is teleologically
independent **L**(**MN**)-for-**J**[b] for person y **K**(**FG**)-for-**H**[a]
in time-interval τ"
  "DLB_SPC_TL_PRS(x,**L**{**M**, . . . ,**N**,**J**[b]} [x];y,**K**{**F**,
  . . . ,**G**,**H**[a]} [y];τ)" = df.
  "SPC_TL_PRS(x,**L**{**M**, . . . ,**N**,**J**[b]} [x];y,**K**{**F**,
  . . . ,**G**,**H**[a]} [y];τ) & V_BLF_(SPC_TL_PRS(x,**L**{**M**,
  . . . ,**N**,**J**[b]} [x];y,**K**{**F**, . . . ,**G**,**H**[a]} [y];τ), x,τ)"

SOC 31   "x is a person who is deliberately teleologically independent
L(**MN**)-for-**H**[a] convergently for person y **K**(**FG**)-for-**H**[a]
in time-interval τ" = df.
"x is a person who is deliberately teleologically independent
L(**MN**)-for-**H**[a] for person y **K**(**FG**)-for-**H**[a] in time-
interval τ"
  "CNV_DLB_SPC_TL_PRS(x,**L**{**M**, . . . ,**N**,**H**[a]}
  [x];y,**K**{**F**, . . . ,**G**,**H**[a]} [y];τ)" = df.
  "DLB_SPC_TL_PRS(x,**L**{**M**, . . . ,**N**,**H**[a]} [x];y,**K**{**F**,
  . . . ,**G**,**H**[a]} [y];τ)"

SOC 32   "x is a person who is deliberately teleologically independent
           K(FG)-for-**J**[b] divergently for person y **K(FG)**-for-**H**[a] in
           time-interval τ" = df.
           "x is a person who is deliberately teleologically independent
           K(FG)-for-**J**[b] for person y **K(FG)**-for-**H**[a] in time-
           interval τ"
           "DIV_DLB_SPC_TL_PRS(x,**K**{**F**, . . . ,**G**,**J**[b]} [x];y,**K**{**F**,
           . . . ,**G**,**H**[a]} [y];τ)" = df.
           "DLB_SPC_TL_PRS(x,**K**{**F**, . . . ,**G**,**J**[b]} [x];y,**K**{**F**,
           . . . ,**G**,**H**[a]} [y];τ)"

SOC 33   "x is a person who is deliberately teleologically independent
           K(FG)-for-**H**[a] in concert for person y in time-interval τ"
           = df.
           "x is a person who is deliberately teleologically independent
           K(FG)-for-**H**[a] with person y **K(FG)**-for-**H**[a] in time-
           interval τ"
           "DLB_SPC_TL_PRS_CCR(x,**K**{**F**, . . . ,**G**,**H**[a]} [x],y; τ)"
           = df.
           "DLB_SPC_TL_PRS(x,**K**{**F**, . . . ,**G**,**H**[a]} y,**K**{**F**,
           . . . ,**G**,**H**[a]} [y];τ)"

SOC 34   "x and y symmetrically mutually cooperate **L(MN)**-for-**J**[b],
           K(FG)-for-**H**[a], in time-interval τ" = df.
           "x is a person who cooperates **L(MN)**-for-**J**[b] with person y
           K(FG)-for-**H**[a] in time-interval τ *and* y is a person who
           cooperates **K(FG)**-for-**H**[a] with person x **L(MN)**-for-**J**[b]
           in time-interval τ"
           "SYM_MUT_SPC_CP_PRSS(x,**L**{**M**, . . . ,**N**,**J**[b]}
           [x];y,**K**{**F**, . . . ,**G**,**H**[a]} [y];τ)" = df.
           "SPC_CP_PRS(x,**L**{**M**, . . . ,**N**,**J**[b]} [x];y,**K**{**F**,
           . . . ,**G**,**H**[a]} [y];τ) & SPC_CP_PRS(y,**K**{**F**, . . . ,
           G,**H**[a]} [y];x,**L**{**M**, . . . ,**N**,**J**[b]} [x];τ)"

SOC 35   "x and y symmetrically mutually cooperate **L(MN)**-for-**H**[a],
           K(FG)-for-**H**[a], convergently in time-interval τ" = df.
           "x and y symmetrically mutually cooperate **L(MN)**-for-**H**[a],
           K(FG)-for-**H**[a], in time-interval τ"
           "CNV_SYM_MUT_SPC_CP_PRSS(x,**L**{**M**, . . . ,**N**,**H**[a]}
           [x];y,**K**{**F**, . . . ,**G**,**H**[a]} [y];τ)" = df.

"SYM_MUT_SPC_CP_PRSS(x,**L**{**M**, . . . ,**N**,**H**[a]}
[x];y,**K**{**F**, . . . ,**G**,**H**[a]} [y];τ)"

SOC 36   "x and y symmetrically mutually cooperate **K**(**FG**)-for-**J**[b],
K(**FG**)-for-**H**[a], divergently in time-interval τ" = df.
"x and y symmetrically mutually cooperate **K**(**FG**)-for-**J**[b],
K(**FG**)-for-**H**[a], in time-interval τ"
"DIV_SYM_MUT_SPC_CP_PRSS(x,**K**{**F**, . . . ,**G**,**J**[b]}
[x];y,**K**{**F**, . . . ,**G**,**H**[a]} [y];τ)" = df.
"SYM_MUT_SPC_CP_PRSS(x,**K**{**F**, . . . ,**G**,**J**[b]}
[x];y,**K**{**F**, . . . ,**G**,**H**[a]} [y];τ)"

SOC 37   "x and y symmetrically mutually cooperate **K**(**FG**)-for-**H**[a] in
concert in time-interval τ" = df.
"x and y symmetrically mutually cooperate **K**(**FG**)-for-**H**[a],
K(**FG**)-for-**H**[a], in time-interval τ"
"SYM_MUT_SPC_CP_PRSS_CCR(x,**K**{**F**, . . . ,**G**,**H**[a]}
[x];y,**K**{**F**, . . . ,**G**,**H**[a]} [y];τ)" = df.
"SYM_MUT_SPC_CP_PRSS(x,**K**{**F**, . . . ,**G**,**H**[a]}
[x];y,**K**{**F**, . . . ,**G**,**H**[a]} [y];τ)"

SOC 38   "x and y symmetrically mutually conflict **L**(**MN**)-for-**J**[b],
K(**FG**)-for-**H**[a], in time-interval τ" = df.
"x is a person who conflicts **L**(**MN**)-for-**J**[b] with person y
K(**FG**)-for-**H**[a] in time-interval τ *and* y is a person who
conflicts **K**(**FG**)-for-**H**[a] with person x **L**(**MN**)-for-**J**[b] in
time-interval τ"
"SYM_MUT_SPC_CF_PRSS(x,**L**{**M**, . . . ,**N**,**J**[b]}
[x];y,**K**{**F**, . . . ,**G**,**H**[a]} [y];τ)" = df.
"SPC_CF_PRS(x,**L**{**M**, . . . ,**N**,**J**[b]} [x];y,**K**{**F**,
. . . ,**G**,**H**[a]} [y];τ) & SPC_CF_PRS(y,**K**{**F**, . . . ,
G,**H**[a]} [y];x,**L**{**M**, . . . ,**N**,**J**[b]} [x];τ)"

SOC 39   "x and y symmetrically mutually conflict **L**(**MN**)-for-**H**[a],
K(**FG**)-for-**H**[a], convergently in time-interval τ" = df.
"x and y symmetrically mutually conflict **L**(**MN**)-for-**H**[a],
K(**FG**)-for-**H**[a], in time-interval τ"
"CNV_SYM_MUT_SPC_CF_PRSS(x,**L**{**M**, . . . ,**N**,**H**[a]}
[x];y,**K**{**F**, . . . ,**G**,**H**[a]} [y];τ)" = df.
"SYM_MUT_SPC_CF_PRSS(x,**L**{**M**, . . . ,**N**,**H**[a]}
[x];y,**K**{**F**, . . . ,**G**,**H**[a]} [y];τ)"

SOC 40   "x and y symmetrically mutually conflict **K**(**FG**)-for-**J**[b],
          K(**FG**)-for-**H**[a], divergently in time-interval τ" = df.
          "x and y symmetrically mutually conflict **K**(**FG**)-for-**J**[b],
          K(**FG**)-for-**H**[a], in time-interval τ"
               "DIV_SYM_MUT_SPC_CF_PRSS(x,**K**{**F**, . . . ,**G**,**J**[b]}
               [x];y,**K**{**F**, . . . ,**G**,**H**[a]} [y];τ)" = df.
               "SYM_MUT_SPC_CF_PRSS(x,**K**{**F**, . . . ,**G**,**J**[b]}
               [x];y,**K**{**F**, . . . ,**G**,**H**[a]} [y];τ)"

SOC 41   "x and y are in symmetric mutual competition **K**(**FG**)-for-**H**[a]
          in time-interval τ" = df.
          "x and y symmetrically mutually conflict **K**(**FG**)-for-**H**[a],
          K(**FG**)-for-**H**[a], in time-interval τ"
               "SYM_MUT_SPC_CPT_PRSS(x,**K**{**F**, . . . ,**G**,**H**[a]}
               [x];y,**K**{**F**, . . . ,**G**,**H**[a]} [y];τ)" = df.
               "SYM_MUT_SPC_CF_PRSS(x,**K**{**F**, . . . ,**G**,**H**[a]}
               [x];y,**K**{**F**, . . . ,**G**,**H**[a]} [y];τ)"

SOC 42   "x and y symmetrically mutually conflict **K**(**FG**)-for-**H**[a],
          K(**FG**)-for-not-**H**[a], head-on in time-interval τ" = df.
          "x and y symmetrically mutually conflict **K**(**FG**)-for-**H**[a],
          K(**FG**)-for-not-**H**[a], in time-interval τ"
               "SYM_MUT_H_ON_SPC_CF_PRSS(x,**K**{**F**, . . . ,**G**,**H**[a]}
               [x];y,**K**{**F**, . . . ,**G**, $-$ **H**[a]} [y];τ)" = df.
               "SYM_MUT_SPC_CF_PRSS(x,**K**{**F**, . . . ,**G**,**H**[a]}
               [x];y,**K**{**F**, . . . ,**G**, $-$ **H**[a]} [y];τ)"

SOC 43   "x and y are symmetrically mutually teleologically independent
          L(**MN**)-for-**J**[b], **K**(**FG**)-for-**H**[a], in time-interval τ" = df.
          "x is a person who is teleologically independent **L**(**MN**)-for-
          J[b] with person y **K**(**FG**)-for-**H**[a] in time-interval τ *and* y is
          a person who is teleologically independent **K**(**FG**)-for-**H**[a]
          with person x **L**(**MN**)-for-**J**[b] in time-interval τ"
               "SYM_MUT_SPC_TL_PRSS(x,**L**{**M**, . . . ,**N**,**J**[b]}
               [x];y,**K**{**F**, . . . ,**G**,**H**[a]} [y];τ)" = df.
               "SPC_TL_PRS(x,**L**{**M**, . . . ,**N**,**J**[b]} [x];y,**K**{**F**,
               . . . ,**G**,**H**[a]} [y];τ) & SPC_TL_PRS(x,**K**{**F**, . . . ,
               G,**H**[a]} [y];x,**L**{**M**, . . . ,**N**,**J**[b]} [x];τ)"

SOC 44   "x and y are symmetrically mutually teleologically independent
          L(**MN**)-for-**H**[a], **K**(**FG**)-for-**H**[a], convergently in time-
          interval τ" = df.

"x and y are symmetrically mutually teleologically independent
L(**MN**)-for-**H**[a], **K**(**FG**)-for-**H**[a], in time-interval τ"
   "CNV_SYM_MUT_SPC_TL_PRSS(x,**L**{**M**, . . . ,**N**,**H**[a]}
   [x];y,**K**{**F**, . . . ,**G**,**H**[a]} [y];τ)" = df.
   "SYM_MUT_SPC_TL_PRSS(x,**L**{**M**, . . . ,**N**,**H**[a]}
   [x];y,**K**{**F**, . . . ,**G**,**H**[a]} [y];τ)"

SOC 45 "x and y are symmetrically mutually teleologically independent
K(**FG**)-for-**J**[b], **K**(**FG**)-for-**H**[a], divergently in time-
interval τ" = df.
"x and y are symmetrically mutually teleologically independent
K(**FG**)-for-**J**[b], **K**(**FG**)-for-**H**[a], in time-interval τ"
   "DIV_SYM_MUT_SPC_TL_PRSS(x,**K**{**F**, . . . ,**G**,**J**[b]}
   [x];y,**K**{**F**, . . . ,**G**,**H**[a]} [y];τ)" = df.
   "SYM_MUT_SPC_TL_PRSS(x,**K**{**F**, . . . ,**G**,**J**[b]}
   [x];y,**K**{**F**, . . . ,**G**,**H**[a]} [y];τ)"

SOC 46 "x and y are symmetrically mutually teleologically independent
K(**FG**)-for-**H**[a], **K**(**FG**)-for-**H**[a], in concert in time-
interval τ" = df.
"x and y are symmetrically mutually teleologically independent
K(**FG**)-for-**H**[a], **K**(**FG**)-for-**H**[a], in time-interval τ"
   "SYM_MUT_SPC_TL_CCR_PRSS(x,**K**{**F**, . . . ,**G**,**H**[a]}
   [x];y,**K**{**F**, . . . ,**G**,**H**[a]} [y];τ)" = df.
   "SYM_MUT_SPC_TL_PRSS(x,**K**{**F**, . . . ,**G**,**H**[a]}
   [x];y,**K**{**F**, . . . ,**G**,**H**[a]} [y];τ)"

SOC 47 "x **L**(**MN**)-for-**J**[b] *and* **K**(**FG**)-for-**H**[a], *and* y **O**(**PQ**)-
for-**I**[c] *and* **R**(**ST**)-for-**U**[d], are persons who are quasi-
symmetrically mutually cooperating in time-interval τ" = df.
"x is a person who cooperates **L**(**MN**)-for-**H**[a] with person y
K(**FG**)-for-**H**[a] in time-interval τ *and* y is a person who
cooperates **O**(**PQ**)-for-**I**[c] with person x **R**(**ST**)-for-**U**[d] in
time-interval τ"
   "Q_SYM_MUT_SPC_CP_PRSS(x,**L**{**M**, . . . ,**N**,**H**[a]}
   [x];y,**L**{**M**, . . . ,**N**,**J**[b]} [y];y,**O**{**P**, . . . ,**Q**,**I**[c]}
   [y];x,**R**{**S**, . . . ,**T**,**U**[d]} [x];τ)" = df.
   "SPC_CP_PRS(x,**L**{**M**, . . . ,**N**,**H**[a]} [x];y,**K**{**F**,
   . . . ,**G**,**H**[a]} [y];τ) & SPC_CP_PRS(x,**O**{**P**, . . . ,
   Q,**I**[c]} [x];y,**R**{**S**, . . . ,**T**,**U**[d]} [y];τ)"

SOC 48   "x **L(MN)**-for-**J**[b] *and* **L(MN)**-for-**H**[a], *and* y **O(PQ)**-
for-**I**[c] *and* **O(PQ)**-for-**F**[d], are persons who are quasi-
symmetrically mutually conflicting divergently in time-interval τ"
= df.

"x is a person who conflicts **L(MN)**-for-**J**[b] divergently with
person y **L(MN)**-for-**H**[a] in time-interval τ *and* y is a person
who conflicts **O(PQ)**-for-**I**[c] divergently with person x
O(PQ)-for-**F**[d] in time-interval τ"

> "Q_SYM_MUT_CONF_DIV_SPC_CF_PRSS(x,**L**{**M**, . . . ,
> **N**,**J**[b]} [x];y,**L**{**M**, . . . ,**N**,**H**[a]} [y];y,**O**{**P**, . . . ,
> **Q**,**I**[c]} [y];x,**O**{**P**, . . . ,**Q**,**F**[d]} [x];τ)" = df.
> "DIV_SPC_CF_PRS(x,**L**{**M**, . . . ,**N**,**J**[b]} [x];y,**L**{**M**,
> . . . ,**N**,**H**[a]} [y];τ) & DIV_SPC_CF_PRS(y,**O**{**P**,
> . . . ,**Q**,**I**[c]} [y];x,**O**{**P**, . . . ,**Q**,**F**[d]} [x];τ)"

SOC 49   "x and y are asymmetrically mutually interacting persons, x
cooperating **L(MN)**-for-**J**[b] with y **K(FG)**-for-**J**[b]
convergently, y conflicting **R(ST)**-for-not-**F**[d] with x **R(ST)**-
for-**F**[d] head-on in time-interval τ" = df.

"x is a person who cooperates **L(MN)**-for-**J**[b] convergently
with person y **K(FG)**-for-**J**[b] in time-interval τ *and* y is a
person who is in head-on conflict **R(ST)**-for-not-**F**[d] with
person x **R(ST)**-for-**F**[d] in time-interval τ"

> "ASYM_MUT_INTR_PRSS_CNV_CONFL(x,**L**{**M**,
> . . . ,**N**,**J**[b]} [x];y,**K**{**F**, . . . ,**G**,**J**[b]} [y],τ; y,**R**{**S**,
> . . . ,**T**, − **F**[d]} [y];x,**R**{**S**, . . . ,**T**,**F**[d]} [x];τ)" = df.
> "CNV_SPC_CP_PRS(x,**L**{**M**, . . . ,**N**,**J**[b]} [x];y,**K**{**F**,
> . . . ,**G**,**J**[b]} [y],τ) & H_ON_SPC_CF_PRS(y,**R**{**S**,
> . . . ,**T**, − **F**[d]} [y];x,**R**{**S**, . . . ,**T**,**F**[d]} [y];τ)"

SOC 50   "x and y are **K(FG)**-for-**H**[a] rivals in time-interval τ" = df.
"x and y are in symmetric mutual competition **K(FG)**-for-**H**[a]
in time-interval τ *or* x and y satisfy an index of: x *and* y are in
symmetric mutual competition **K(FG)**-for-**H**[a] in time-interval
τ"

> "SPC_RVS(x,y,**K**{**F**, . . . ,**G**,**H**[a]} [x,y];τ)" = df.
> "SYM_MUT_SPC_CPT_PRSS(x,**K**{**F**, . . . ,**G**,**H**[a]}
> [x];y,**K**{**F**, . . . ,**G**,**H**[a]} [y];τ) ᵛ
> IX(SYM_MUT_SPC_CPT_PRSS(x,**K**{**F**, . . . ,**G**,**H**[a]}
> [x];y,**K**{**F**, . . . ,**G**,**H**[a]} [y];τ),(x & y),τ″)"

SOC 51   "person x takes revenge on person y in time-interval τ'" = df.
"τ is an earlier-and-discrete time-interval relative to τ' *and* y is a
person who conflicts with person x in time-interval τ *and* x is a
person who deliberately conflicts with person y in time-interval
τ'"
   "RVNG(x,y,τ)" = df.
   "EDT(τ,τ') & CF_PRS_WITH_PRS(x,y,τ) &
   DLB_CF_PRS(x,y,τ')"

SOC 52   "person x avenges person z on person y in time-interval τ" = df.
"τ is an earlier-and-discrete time-interval relative to τ' *and* y is a
person who conflicts with person z in time-interval τ *and* x is a
person who deliberately conflicts with person y in time-interval
τ'"
   "AVNG(x,z,y,τ)" = df.
   "EDT(τ,τ') & CF_PRS_WITH_PRS(y,z,τ) &
   DLB_CF_PRS(x,y,τ')"

SOC 53   "person x makes a certain **K(FG)**-for-**H**[a] investment in time-
interval τ with person y **L(MN)**-for-**J**[b] in time-interval τ'"
= df.
"x is a person who cooperates **K(FG)**-for-**H**[a] with person y
L(MN)-for-**J**[b] in time-interval τ *and* person x expects, in
time-interval τ, that y is a person who cooperates **L(MN)**-for-
J[b] with person x **K(FG)**-for-**H**[a] in time-interval τ'"
   "SPC_CRT_INV(x,**K**{**F**, . . . ,**G**,**H**[a]} [x], τ;y,**L**{**M**,
      . . . ,**N**,**J**[b]} [y],τ')" = df.
   "SPC_CP_PRS(x,**K**{**F**, . . . ,**G**,**H**[a]} [x];y,**L**{**M**,
      . . . ,**N**,**J**[b]} [y];τ) &
   XPC_EVNT(x,τ,SPC_CP_PRS(y,**L**{**M**, . . . ,**N**,**J**[b]}
   [y];x,**K**{**F**, . . . ,**G**,**H**[a]} [x];τ'),τ)"

SOC 54   "persons x and y enter into a **K(FG)**-for-**H**[a]-time-τ',
L(MN)-for-**J**[b]-time-τ'', agreement, in time-interval τ" = df.
"τ is an earlier-and-discrete time-interval relative to τ' *and* τ is an
earlier-and-discrete time-interval relative to τ'' *and* person x
states, at time τ, that x plans to cooperate **L(MN)**-for-**J**[b] with
person y, **K(FG)**-for-**H**[a] at time τ' *and* person x states, at
time τ, that x expects person y to cooperate **K(FG)**-for-**H**[a]
with person x **L(MN)**-for-**J**[b] at time τ'' *and* person y states,
at time τ, that y plans to cooperate **K(FG)**-for-**H**[a] with

person x, **L**(**MN**)-for-**J**[b] at time τ'' *and* y expects person x to cooperate **L**(**MN**)-for-**J**[b] with person y **K**(**FG**)-for-**H**[a] at time τ'"

"SPC_AGR(x,**L**{**M**, . . . ,**N**,**J**[b]} [x],τ';y,**K**{**F**, . . . ,**G**,**H**[a]} [y],τ'',τ)" = df.

"EDT(τ,τ') & EDT(τ,τ'') & STS(x,PL_EXH_B_BEH(x,τ,SPC_CP_PRS(x,**L**{**M**, . . . ,**N**,**J**[b]} [x];y,**K**{**F**, . . . ,**G**,**H**[a]} [y];τ'),τ'),y,τ) & STS(x,XPC_EVNT(x,τ,SPC_CP_PRS(y,**K**{**F**, . . . , **G**,**H**[a]} [y];x,**L**{**M**, . . . ,**N**,**J**[b]} [x];τ''),τ''),y,τ) & STS(y,PL_EXH_B_BEH(y,τ,SPC_CP_PRS(y,**K**{**F**, . . . ,**G**,**H**[a]} [y];x,**L**{**M**, . . . ,**N**,**J**[b]} [x];τ''),τ''),x,τ) & STS(y,XPC_EVNT(y,τ,SPC_CP_PRS x,**L**{**M**, . . . ,**N**,**J**[b]} [x];y,**K**{**F**, . . . ,**G**,**H**[a]} [y];τ'),τ'),x,τ)"

SOC 55 "person x pays **K**(**FG**)-for-**H**[y] to person y in time-interval τ" = df.

"y is a person who conflicts **K**(**FG**)-for-**H**[y] with person x **K**(**FG**)-for-**H**[y] in time-interval τ *and* x is a person who cooperates **K**(**FG**)-for-**H**[y] with person y **K**(**FG**)-for-**H**[y] in time-interval τ"

"SPC_PAY(x,y,**K**{**F**, . . . ,**G**,**H**[y]} [x];τ)" = df.

"SPC_CF_PRS(y,**K**{**F**, . . . ,**G**,**H**[y]} [y];x,**K**{**F**, . . . ,**G**,**H**[y]} [x];τ) & SPC_CP_PRS(x,**K**{**F**, . . . , **G**,**H**[y]} [x];y,**K**{**F**, . . . , **G**,**H**[y]} [y];τ)"

SOC 56 "person x trades **H** in time-interval τ to person y for **J** in time-interval τ'" = df.

"person x pays **K**(**FG**)-for-**H**[y] to person y in time-interval τ *and* person y pays **L**(**MN**)-for-**J**[x] to person x in time-interval τ'"

"TRD(x,**H**,τ;y,**J**,τ')" = df.

"SPC_PAY(x,y,**K**{**F**, . . . ,**G**,**H**[y]} [x];τ) & SPC_PAY(y,x,**L**{**M**, . . . ,**N**,**J**[x]} [y];τ')"

SOC 57 "persons x and y enter into a **K**(**FG**)-for-**H**[a]-time-τ', **L**(**MN**)-for-**J**[b]-time-τ'', contract, in time-interval τ, with penalties **R**(**ST**)-for-**U**[c], **O**(**PQ**)-for-**V**[d]" = df.

"persons x and y enter into a **K**(**FG**)-for-**H**[a]-time-τ', **L**(**MN**)-for-**J**[b]-time-τ'', agreement, in time-interval τ *and* if, in time-interval τ', x does not cooperate **L**(**MN**)-for-**J**[b] with

person y **K(FG)**-for-**H**[a] then person x pays **R(ST)**-for-
U[y] to person y in time-interval τ', *and* if, in time-interval τ'', y
does not cooperate **K(FG)**-for-**H**[a] with person x **L(MN)**-
for-**J**[b] then person y pays **O(PQ)**-for-**V**[x] to person x in
time-interval τ'''"

"SPC_CTR(x,**L{M**, . . . ,**N,J**[b]} [x];**R{S**, . . . ,**T,U**[y]}
[x],τ';y,**K{F**, . . . ,**G,H**[a]} [y],**O{P**, . . . ,**Q,V**[x]}
[y];τ'')" = df.

"SPC_AGR(x,**L{M**, . . . ,**N,J**[b]} [x],τ';y,**K{F**,
 . . . ,**G,H**[a]} [y];τ';τ) & (− SPC_CP_PRS(x,**L{M**,
 . . . ,**N,J**[b]} [x];τ') ⊃ SPC_PAY(x,y,**R{S**, . . . ,**T,U**[y]}
[x],τ')) & (− SPC_CP_PRS(y,**K{F**, . . . ,**G,H**[a]} [y];τ'')
⊃ SPC_PAY(y,x,**O{P**, ... ,**Q,V**[x]} [y];τ'))"

Bibliography

Russell L. Ackoff. *See* C. West Churchman and Russell L. Ackoff.

[1]   Kenneth J. Arrow. *Social Choice and Individual Values.* Cowles Commission Monograph 12. New York: Jhn Wiley and Sons, Inc., 1951.

[2]   Kenneth J. Arrow and Frank H. Hahn. *General Competitive Analysis.* San Francisco: Holden-Day, 1971.

Robert B. Barrett. *See* Robert J. Wolfson and Robert B. Barrett.

[3]   Robert B. Barrett, Richard S. Rudner, and Robert J. Wolfson. *Organizational Decision-Making: A Constructionalist Approach.* D-14850-PR. Santa Monica, Calif.: The RAND Corporation, June 1966.

Jim Boyle. *See* Larry Wos, Ross Overbeek, Ewing Lusk, and Jim Boyle.

[4]   Percival W. Bridgman. *Dimensional Analysis.* New Haven: Yale University Press, 1922.

Donald T. Campbell. *See* Robert A. LeVine and Donald T. Campbell.

[5]   Rudolf Carnap. *Der Logische Aufbau der Welt.* Berlin, 1928. English translation: *The Logical Structure of the World,* trans. Rolf A. George. Berkeley: University of California Press, 1967.

[6]   ———. *Introduction to Symbolic Logic and Its Applications.* Vienna, 1954. (New York: Dover Press, 1958).

[7]   Chin-Liang Chang and Richard Char-Tung Lee. *Symbolic Logic and Mechanical Theorem Proving.* New York: Academic Press, 1973.

[8]   Philip Dormer Stanhope [Lord Chesterfield]. *Lord Chesterfield's Advice to His Son.* New Brunswick, N.J.: printed by Abraham Blauvelt, 1801.

[9]   C. West Churchman and Russell L. Ackoff. *Psychologistics.* University of Pennsylvania (mimeo), 1947.

[10] ———. "An Experimental Definition of Personality." *Philosophy of Science* 14 (1947): 304–32.

[11] Clyde H. Coombs. "A Theory of Psychological Scaling." *Engineering Research Bulletin,* no. 54. University of Michigan, Ann Arbor, 1952.

———. *See* Robert M. Thrall, Clyde H. Coombs, and Robert L. Davis.

[12] Richard H. Cyert and James G. March. *A Behavioral Theory of the Firm.* Englewood Cliffs, N.J.: Prentice-Hall, 1963.

[13] Paul Davidson. *Money and the Real World.* 2d ed. London: Macmillan, 1978. Robert L. Davis. *See* Robert M. Thrall, Clyde H. Coombs, and Robert L. Davis.

[14] Stuart Carter Dodd. *Dimensions of Society.* New York: The Macmillan Company, 1942.

[15] David Easton. *The Political System.* New York: Alfred A. Knopf and Co., 1953.

[16] ———. *A Framework for Political Analysis.* Englewood Cliffs,' N.J.: Prentice-Hall, 1965.

[17] ———. *A Systems Analysis of Political Life.* New York: John Wiley and Sons, Inc., 1965.

[18] Alfred S. Eichner. *The Megacorp and Oligopoly.* Cambridge: Cambridge University Press, 1976.

[19] Paul K. Feyerabend. "Explanation, Reduction and Empiricism." In Herbert Feigl and Grover Maxwell, eds., *Minnesota Studies in the Philosophy of Science.* Minneapolis: University of Minnesota Press, 1962, 3:28–97.

[20] Hartry H. Field. *Science without Numbers: A Defence of Nominalism.* Oxford: Basil Blackwell, 1980.
Arthur S. Goldberger. *See* Lawrence R. Klein and Arthur S. Goldberger.

[21] Nelson Goodman. "A World of Individuals." In I. M. Bochenski, A. Church, and N. Goodman, eds., *The Problem of Universals.* South Bend, Ind.: University of Notre Dame Press, 1956, pp. 13–31.

[22] ———. "The Test of Simplicity." *Science* 128 (1958): 1064–69.

[23] ———. "Recent Developments in the Theory of Simplicity." *Philosophy and Phenomenological Research* 19 (1959): 429–46.

[24] ———. *Fact, Fiction and Forecast.* 3d ed. Indianapolis: Bobbs-Merrill, 1973.

[25] ———. *The Structure of Appearance.* 3d ed. Dordrecht, Holland, and Boston, Mass.: D. Reidel Publishing Co., 1977.
Nelson Goodman. *See* Henry S. Leonard and Nelson Goodman.

[26] Nelson Goodman and W. V. O. Quine. "Steps toward a Constructive Nominalism." *Journal of Symbolic Logic* 12 (1947): 105–22.

[27] Bertram M. Gross. *Organizations and Their Management.* New York: The Free Press, 1968.
Frank H. Hahn. *See* Kenneth J. Arrow and Frank H. Hahn.

[28] Melvin Hausner. "Multidimensional Utilities." In [67], 167–80.

[29] Carl G. Hempel. *Aspects of Scientific Explanation and Other Essays.* New York: The Free Press, 1965.

[30] *International Encyclopedia of Unified Science.* Chicago: University of Chicago Press. Vol. 1, 1955. Vol. 2, 1970.
Abraham Kaplan. *See* Harold D. Lasswell and Abraham Kaplan.

[31] Lawrence R. Klein and Arthur S. Goldberger. *An Econometric Model of the United States, 1929–1952.* Amsterdam: North-Holland Publishing Co., 1955.

[32] Jan A. Kregel. *Rate of Profit, Distribution and Growth: Two Views.* Chicago: Aldine, 1971.

[33] ———. *The Reconstruction of Political Economy.* New York: Halsted, 1973.

[34]   Kelvin Lancaster. *Consumer Demand*. New York: Columbia University Press, 1971.

[35]   Harold D. Lasswell and Abraham Kaplan. *Power and Society: A Framework for Political Inquiry*. New Haven: Yale University Press, 1950.

[36]   Henry S. Leonard and Nelson Goodman. "The Calculus of Individuals and Its Uses." *Journal of Symbolic Logic* 5 (1940): 44–55.

[37]   Robert A. LeVine and Donald T. Campbell. *Ethnocentrism: Theories of Conflict, Ethnic Attitudes, and Group Behavior*. New York: John Wiley and Sons, Inc., 1972.

[38]   David K. Lewis. *Convention: A Philosophical Study*. Cambridge: Harvard University Press, 1969.

[39]   R. Duncan Luce and Howard Raiffa. *Games and Decisions*. New York: John Wiley and Sons, Inc., 1957.

       Ewing Lusk. *See* Larry Wos, Ross Overbeek, Ewing Lusk, and Jim Boyle.

[40]   Edmond Malinvaud. *Lectures on Microeconomic Theory*. Amsterdam: North-Holland Publishing Co., 1972.

[41]   James G. March and Herbert A. Simon. *Organizations*. New York: John Wiley and Sons, Inc., 1958.

       James G. March. *See* Richard H. Cyert and James G. March.

[42]   William W. McCune. *Otter 1.0 User's Guide*. Mathematics and Computer Science Division, Argonne National Laboratory, Argonne, Ill., 1989.

[43]   Hyman P. Minsky. *John Maynard Keynes*. New York: Columbia University Press, 1975.

[44]   ———. *Can "It" Happen Again?* Armonk, N.Y.: M. E. Sharpe, Inc., 1982.

[45]   ———. *Stabilizing an Unstable Economy*. New Haven: Yale University Press, 1986.

[46]   Philip Mirowski. "Physics and the 'Marginalist Revolution.'" *Cambridge Journal of Economics* 8 (1984): 361–79.

[47]   ———, ed. *The Reconstruction of Economic Theory*. Boston: Kluwer-Nijhoff, 1986.

[48]   ———. *Against Mechanism: Protecting Economics from Science*. Totowa, N.J.: Rowman & Littlefield, 1988.

[49]   ———. *More Heat than Light: Economics as Social Physics, Physics as Nature's Economics*. New York: Cambridge University Press, 1989.

[50]   *The Monist*.

[51]   Nils J. Nilsson. *Problem-Solving Methods in Artificial Intelligence*. New York: McGraw-Hill, 1971.

       Ross Overbeek. *See* Larry Wos, Ross Overbeek, Ewing Lusk, and Jim Boyle.

[52]   *Compact Edition of the Oxford English Dictionary*. Oxford: Oxford University Press, 1971.

[53]   Talcott Parsons. *The Social System*. Glencoe, Ill.: The Free Press, 1951.

[54]   Talcott Parsons, Edward A. Shils, et al. *Notes toward a General Theory of Action*. Cambridge: Harvard University Press, 1951.

[55]   Talcott Parsons and Neil J. Smelser. *Economy and Society*. Glencoe, Ill.: The Free Press, 1956.

[56]   Charles Perrow. *Complex Organizations: A Critical Essay*. 3d ed. New York: Random House, 1986.

[57] Jeffrey Pfeffer. *Organizations and Organization Theory*. Boston: Pitman Publishing, Inc., 1982.

W. V. O. Quine. *See* Nelson Goodman and W. V. O. Quine.

Howard Raiffa. *See* R. Duncan Luce and Howard Raiffa.

[58] Richard Rorty, ed. *The Linguistic Turn: Recent Essays in Philosophical Method*. Edited and with an Introduction by Richard Rorty. Chicago: University of Chicago Press, 1967.

Richard S. Rudner. *See* Robert B. Barrett, Richard S. Rudner, and Robert J. Wolfson.

[59] Richard S. Rudner. *Philosophy of Social Science*. Prentice-Hall Foundations of Philosophy Series, Elizabeth and Monroe Beardsley, eds. Englewood Cliffs, N.J.: Prentice-Hall, Inc., 1966.

[60] Richard S. Rudner and Robert J. Wolfson. "Notes on a Constructional Framework for a Theory of Organizational Decision Making." In Norman F. Washburne, ed., *Decisions, Values and Groups*. New York: Pergamon Press, 1962, pp. 371–409.

Bertrand Russell. *See* Alfred North Whitehead and Bertrand Russell.

[61] Paul A. Samuelson. *Foundations of Economic Analysis*. Cambridge, Mass.: Harvard University Press, 1948.

[62] Amartya K. Sen. *Collective Choice and Social Welfare*. San Francisco: Holden-Day, 1970.

[63] William Shakespeare. *Hamlet, the Prince of Denmark*. In *The Tragedies of Shakespeare*. The Modern Library. New York: Random House.

Edward A. Shils. *See* Talcott Parsons, Edward A. Shils, et al.

Neil J. Smelser. *See* Talcott Parsons and Neil J. Smelser.

[64] Adam Smith. *The Theory of Moral Sentiments* (1759). Glasgow: University of Glasgow, 1976.

[65] ———. *An Inquiry into the Nature and Causes of "The Wealth of Nations"* (1776). Edited and with an Introduction by Edwin Cannan. New York: Modern Library, 1937.

[66] S. S. Stevens. "Mathematics, Measurement, and Psychophysics." In S. S. Stevens, ed., *Handbook of Experimental Psychology*. New York: John Wiley and Sons, Inc., 1950.

[67] Robert M. Thrall, Clyde H. Coombs, and Robert L. Davis, eds. *Decision Processes*. New York: John Wiley and Sons, Inc., 1954.

[68] Robert M. Thrall. "Applications of Multidimensional Utility Theory." [67], 181–86.

[69] Max Weber. *Economy and Society*. Edited by Guenther Roth and Claus Wittich. Berkeley and Los Angeles: University of California Press, 1978.

[70] Alfred North Whitehead and Bertrand Russell. *Principia Mathematica*. Cambridge: Cambridge University Press, 1910. 2d ed., 1927.

[71] Peter Winch. *The Idea of a Social Science and Its Relation to Philosophy*. London: Routledge and Kegan Paul, 1958.

[72] Robert J. Wolfson. "Progress in the Development of a Formal Lexicon for the Social Sciences." *Synthese* 46 (1981): 455–65.

[73] ———. "Development of a Formal Lexicon for the Social Sciences." *The Syracuse Scholar* 3, no.1 (1982): 75–89.

[74]   ———. "A Formal Lexicon for the Social Sciences." In *The CONTA Confer-
        ence,* proceedings of the Conference on Conceptual and Terminological Anal-
        ysis in the Social Sciences, May 24–27, 1981, Bielefeld, Federal Republic of
        Germany. Frankfort, 1982, pp. 301–12.
        ———. *See* Robert B. Barrett, Richard S. Rudner, and Robert J. Wolfson.
        ———. *See* Richard S. Rudner and Robert J. Wolfson.
[75]   Robert J. Wolfson and Robert B. Barrett. "On a Formal Lexicon for the Social
        Sciences." *Nature and System* 4 (1982): 223–34.
[76]   Larry Wos, Ross Overbeek, Ewing Lusk, and Jim Boyle. *Automated Reason-
        ing, Introduction and Applications.* Englewood Cliffs, N.J.: Prentice-Hall,
        Inc., 1984.

Index

Robert J. Wolfson, professor of economics at Syracuse University, earned his degrees at the University of Chicago, a B.S. in mathematics and a master's and doctorate in economics. He has taught at the University of Chicago, Michigan State University, and UCLA, and in 1959–60 he held a Ford Foundation Faculty Fellowship in economics.